33

STORIES TO UPLIFT &

YOU CAN

33 STORIES TO UPLIFT & INSPIRE EVERYDAY PEOPLE

Compiled By Nina Motivates

THIS BOOK BELONGS TO

Copyright

You Can: 33 Stories to Uplift & Inspire Everyday People

Publisher

Anointed Hands Publishing

www.ninamotivates.info

Cover Design by: 727 Marketing https://727marketing.com

Edited by Angela McClain amediting35@gmail.com

ISBN: 978-0-578-73433-0

Dedication/Acknowledgements

This book is dedicated to...YOU!

I want to acknowledge the 33 authors who trusted me with their writing. These authors are amazing human beings, who took time out of their lives to pour into this anthology. I appreciate each and every one of you.

A huge thank you to Shawn Robinson of 727 Marketing for all of your hard work through the entire process.

Thank you to Angela McClain for doing an amazing job editing each story.

Table of Content

Introduction – By Nina Motivates

You Can! Those are two of the most powerful words anyone can say to someone. It gives hope. It gives freedom. It encourages. It pushes others to their goals and dreams. When I first became a motivational speaker, I made a CD (they were popular in 2010) called, "You Can." It told my story of growing up with a "disability." I never call my "difference" a "disability," but for the sake of this piece, I will say the "legal" term.

I discussed how I was born with club hands, meaning my thumbs did not properly develop. Therefore, the doctors had to cut off my thumbs and move all my fingers over one place. My arms are also short and hands are a little twisted. My left hand also has limited mobility. Living with a difference brought challenges, but I have learned I can do anything needed, wanted, or desired! I had challenges, yes! I was bullied as a kid, and an adult. I was discriminated against. I had dating challenges, job challenges, and so much more. Through it all, I learned that if I put my mind to it, I can do it.

Everyone, and I do mean EVERYONE, will have challenges in life. We each will go through some things that will test us and even make us consider giving up. However, if we build ourselves up with the power of "I Can" we will be unstoppable.

In this powerful book, you have 33 authors reminding you that YOU CAN! You will read stories of the different experiences these "everyday people" have gone through. No matter who you are, you go through. The thing is, sometimes you need to be reminded, YOU CAN overcome! YOU CAN win! YOU CAN love you! YOU CAN start over! YOU CAN be successful! YOU CAN! Period!

This book is broken into three parts. Part one is to encourage you to believe. Believe in God, the creator of the universe and everything in it. Believe in you. Believe that YOU CAN. Part two shares stories to push you towards letting go of all you encountered in life, no matter what it was/is. Sometimes we think we are alone. These stories show you, you are not alone. They prove to you that YOU CAN recover! Part three brings it all together. You believe, then you let go, lastly, you soar. Each story in this book is unique to the author life and style of writing. There is something for everyone. Yes, even YOU! Do not miss one story in this book. Be empowered. Take the tools you need and share the ones you do not need with someone who does need it.

I know there is hope in this book for you. I know you will find yourself, or your past in some of the stories. I know you will get something to fuel as you turn the pages of each intimate story. I know by the time you are done reading this anthology, you will know that no matter what, YOU CAN!

Nina Motivates

www.ninamotivates.info

coachninamotivates@gmail.com

All social media @ninamotivates

Part 1 – YOU CAN BELIEVE

You Are Enough

By Willie E. Gant, Jr.

Then the Lord God formed man from the dust of the ground and breathed into his nostrils the breath of life, and the man became a living being. – Genesis 2:7

By the time you finish reading this, I pray that you will understand and begin to accept how amazing and precious you are to God.

You

Several years ago, I was invited to speak at the Mt. Olive Baptist Church in my hometown of Shaw, Mississippi where Reverend Amos C. Gilmore is the pastor. During my time of seeking what God wanted me to speak, He guided me to doing research on the elements that are found in jewelry such as diamonds, pearls, rubies, and so on. Some of those elements are calcium, aluminum, and carbon just to name a few. I then grew interested in re-learning the elements that compose our human bodies, which are oxygen, carbon, hydrogen, calcium, and several others. I was quickly amazed to learn that the riches we desire to have are a part of us. The same way you look at jewelry as beautiful and expensive is the same way God views you. In God's eyes, there is not enough money to match your value. Here's a free one for you: in Genesis 1, the Word says that God spoke everything into existence, but in Genesis 2 God formed humanity. Do you know how special that makes you? If you were a carpenter, you would carefully make furniture with precision. Due to the time and energy put into it, you would do your best to keep it in tip-top shape. God wants you to know that you are His greatest creation, that you are the apple of His eye, and He desires to show you how much He cares for you. Just as King Solomon had everything, a man could imagine having on earth. God who created all things, still wants you, because to Him, nothing compares to you.

Are

I define the word "are" as presently living. Too often when people go through traumatic experiences, they allow those events to dictate their lives. Losing a loved one, being molested, witnessing or experiencing various types of abuse, and being neglected are just a few events that can control a person's life, but only if they allow them to do so. In one of my favorite movies, the main character ran from a promise that his father gave him because of painful events that occurred during his childhood. Throughout the movie, he learned that whatever happened in the past was exactly that, in the past. It did not matter in his present life because he was living right then, not back when. What only really matters is right now. The time you have, the breath you are breathing, the steps you take, the decisions you make. Everything in the past is dead, it has no connection to the present or future, and if you continue to live in the past, you will die as well. The person you were meant to be will not experience life in its fullness. The experiences and opportunities you were to have taken would be missed. What separates you from everything else that God made is that you have the breath of life in you, which is His Spirit. Nowhere else in the Bible can you find where it says that God breathed His Spirit inside of another living being, only in humanity. Basically, you exist because of Him. You are far greater than what you have went through and what others say about you because you are still living!

Enough

When God created humanity, He intentionally wanted us to realize that we are enough. He even waited until He made everything else before we came into the picture. Google defines the word enough as "as much or as many as required," meaning that there is nothing else needed to make it better because it is the standard. Think of it as your favorite meal you love to eat. Whether you cook it or not, all the ingredients that are put into it, satisfy your taste buds, so it really does not matter if someone else does not like it, BECAUSE YOU LOVE IT! No matter how many variations of it you have tasted, it still cannot compare to the original. God knew what and who He wanted you to be before you were formed in your mother's womb. Even before time began, He had you on His mind. Notice how a baby automatically grows into the person they were meant to be over time. It is not forced, because God intended it to be. So, what sense does it make for you to be persuaded by today's culture, fads, or lifestyles when they change at the blink of an eye just to be accepted by people when you were created by God who made everything? If you pay attention, the only things that have remained the same were made by God. The wind still blows; the sun, moon, and stars still shine; plants still grow from the ground; and the earth still rotates on its axis. You had nothing to do with it, but God had everything to do with it. When you face God, He will not search for the physical and materialistic things; He will look at your heart. It is fine to achieve great things in life... go to school, make some money, get a nice ride and home, wear the cool clothes, but never let your identity be wrapped in them because once they are taken away or lost, you will be as well.

In closing, the words in this letter are the very ones I have to remind myself of daily. Yes, there are times when I get down, but I have learned that there is nothing that can encourage and lift me up again but God's Word. To whomever reads this, I pray that you will allow God into your life and accept Jesus as your Savior if you have not done so already. If you have, hold on to God's unchanging hand! Be blessed in Jesus Name!

gantwillie@gmail.com

Why Me? Am I God's Champion? *By Daniel D. Talley*

I was born to two teenage parents and experienced a childhood of poverty where food stamps and welfare were my companions. *Why me, Lord?* As a child, I had a speech impediment and was bullied. *Why me, Lord?* At age 12, I was sexually assaulted by a family member. *Why me, Lord?* As a teenager, I repeated the cycle of my parents and became a parent myself. *Why me, Lord?* I received my high school diploma, but by age 19, I was addicted to drugs. *Why me, Lord?* At age 29, I stole food from a local grocery store to feed my family and received a 3-year prison sentence. *Why me, Lord?* At the age of 41, I found love and married the person of my dreams; only to experience heartbreak one year later as this person would have an adulterous affair, resulting in the birth of a child. *Why me, Lord?* On my 50th birthday, I learned that I had cancer. *Why me, Lord?* By age 61, my oldest child was tragically killed in a car accident. *Why me, Lord?*

These are all real-life examples of bad things that unfortunately people experience every day. Through careful examination of our lives, we can deduce why certain tragedies happen to us. All sin has consequences. Sometimes, there is a dotted line relationship between our sin and the situation that we are experiencing. Other times, there is no correlation. Things just seem to happen. *But why me, Lord?*

If you have never uttered the term, "Why me, Lord?" then you are in rare company, because the vast majority of us are intimately familiar with those three words. But a better question might be: *Why not me?*

Note 2 Self: Our trial is a golden opportunity for us to show God what we are made of. It has been said that you can't have a testimony without a test. So, in an odd kind of way–the test is a blessing.

It is important to note that God will never put more on us than we can bear (1 Corinthians 10:13). By our own devices or by chance, our situation is a test and we are God's warriors for that cause. Remember the story of Job (read the book of Job). Job was a righteous man who loved God and God allowed Satan to take away his health, wealth (dude was rich) and family just to prove to Satan that Job would not turn against God. Job was a pawn in a heavenly game of chess that humanity cannot comprehend. Job was God's Champion in his situation. Could it be, that we too are God's Champions in our situation?

Just imagine the glory that we bring to God when we share our triumphant story with others who are suffering and struggling with that same affliction. They will draw strength and encouragement from the Spirit of God that dwells within us.
James 1:2–4 states the following: "Consider it pure joy, my brothers and sisters, whenever you face trials of many kinds, because you know that the testing of your faith produces perseverance. Let perseverance finish its work so that you may be mature and complete, not lacking anything." In other words, our trials serve a meaningful purpose in our lives and provides an opportunity for a reward.

Did you know this is how we earn one of the available crowns on judgement day? Say what? That's right! The Crown of Life will be given to those who persevere under trials (James 1:12). Wow! We have an opportunity to be one of God's champions.

All you warriors out there, handle your business, and go out and earn your bling-bling! Our Lord is with us!

"The Note 2 Self Guy"

Contact #: 336.253.8769

Email: thenote2selfguy@gmail.com

Website: www.note2selfseries.com

YouTube: The Note 2 Self Guy
Facebook: https://www.facebook.com/Note2SelfGuy/

Twitter/Instagram @Note2SelfGuy

You Can Overcome

By Lauren Ashley Kelly

We make our plans, but the Lord determines our steps. It couldn't be truer in my case. If you would have asked me five years ago what I would be doing with my life, I probably would have said something to the effects of working in retail and making good money. I would not have chosen to be a full-time entrepreneur, owning a successful home daycare, catering company, as well as being a servant leader in ministry. There will be many obstacles that we will face in life, but know that if I could overcome, so can you.

I believe God used the passion I have for cooking for the purpose of personal evangelism and bringing people together. Food is a universal language, and just like Jesus used it to minister and tell of God's goodness, I'm able to do the same. Feeding people spiritually and naturally; caring for the soul through soul food, I have been cooking for over 13 years. As a chef, I have come to learn that education can lead you to a great career but it is the GIFT that God gives you that makes you successful and brings you before great men, Proverbs18:16. Tapping into that gift took pain, struggle, hard work, and support. Success is not easy, but it's worth it. Work hard, connect with the right people, and always acknowledge God as your source.

Although I had both parents in the home, I still felt like something was missing. My father was a hard-working man and strived to always provide for his family. Long hours on the road left little time to actually connect and form an intimate relationship. My mother has been in childcare for most of my life and has owned a home daycare for over 23 years. She worked hard as well, but had personal struggles of her own, as we all do. My parents loved and nurtured us the best way they knew how; yet, I grew into adolescence and early adulthood with the need to try and fill voids that had been created through conversations with the enemy. *You aren't good enough, you're too fat, too bright, nobody wants you, run away, you shouldn't be here, take those pills and just die already,* thoughts that had been formulated in my mind due to molestation and being exposed to sexual abuse. I always had a longing to be good enough, I felt alone even though I had siblings and a huge family, I just never felt like I fit in. This complex caused me to try to fit in even when it became dangerous.

As a child, I didn't understand how these traumas would affect me, but they did. I became toxic and it began to pour out into relationships, friendships, and even looking for love and validation from men. It wasn't until I got down to my lowest that I realized how much I needed God. I remember sitting in a church where I hid in plain sight for years. I heard God speak to me through the man of God preaching. That night I gave my life back to Christ, only He knows what I planned to do when I got home that night. I was tired! Tired of the voices and tired of the feelings of not being enough. God used a few special women in my life to bring me back to life, to bring me back to Him. I took SoulFULLy Smooth catering off the shelf and put it into action through their encouragement. I drove on the expressway after suffering from anxiety through their encouragement. God uses people. That's why you have to be linked up with the right ones.

I started understanding spiritual things, generational curses, and how to break them, deliverance, and what it meant to truly have a personal relationship with God through Christ. I'm grateful God saw fit to place me in a ministry where I can Be Whole, loved, nurtured, and cultivated into who God has called me to be. This is when I realized who I was and what I am made of. I am an overcomer, a champion, a warrior. I didn't always have the same confidence I have now, and it was partly due to struggling with my identity. I know the things I've battled are not just for me but to help free the generations to come. After all, we overcome by the blood of the Lamb and the words of our testimony. Though I loved people in an unhealthy manner before encountering Christ, it has been through people and Godly influences that have helped me to overcome fear, anxiety, idolatry, coercion, depression, and self-doubt. My Apostle and Prophetess always encourage us to apply what we learn. Through practical teaching, I'm able to have successful businesses, nurture my inner man, and maintain my deliverance. I can only pray that my life be a testament of God's grace, mercy, and favor. As you face the fiery trials of life, know that with God on your side, every "set back" can be a set up for a divine comeback! Within the last five years, my life has changed immensely for the better, and I'm forever grateful for the power to overcome! Through prayer, faith, and Godly relationships, I overcame and so can YOU!

Chef Lauren Ashley Kelly

708.595.7116

www.soulfullysmooth.com

www.facebook.com/Soulfullysmooth212

www.instagram.com/soulfully_smooth

Jacob's Ladder – You Can Be Restored From Failure

By Steven Jones

Jacob stepped through the doorway of his two-story, two-car garage, Cape Cod home, carrying his luggage in both arms. For the last six months, it felt like he had been carrying a much heavier load. As he stood at the threshold of the living room, the house seemed different. He astutely recognized that Justine, his wife, an accomplished amateur decorator, had rearranged the furniture and changed the color scheme. Motionless, his eyes did a panoramic movement across the once familiar room and then it hit him; his favorite lounge chair was no longer in the room. He thought to himself: *No wonder this room seemed so much bigger than he remembered.* He was sitting in that chair the night his world got turned upside down. After six months of being away, he painfully attempted to recall the details of that night. Standing next to what appeared to be a new leather sofa, like the kind you see on Wayfair.com or at Ashley furniture, Jacob remembered Justine being so angry with him. She told him she was fed up with his selfish ways and his lack of sensitivity when talking to her; especially with all that she had been dealing with at work. The words came down like a ton of bricks when she told him that she felt like he took her for granted and that he was a terrible communicator. She said, she had put up with it for far too long and she was tired. He remembered sitting in the chair trying to watch the basketball game. What was it that he said to her? He tried hard to remember, but he had been drinking that night too, and he was a little buzzed. That's when he flashed back to one of the many sessions he had with his therapist, when she told him that he had gotten very good at repressing bad memories; that he had been doing it ever since his father left his mother when he was a little boy. He was forced to recall so many bad memories in those sessions, the countless number of tears he cried. He could feel the emotions creeping up in his throat, but he was paralyzed staring into the strange room where the Big Altercation (that's what he had come to call it) occurred. He remembered the tears in his wife's eyes as he yelled at her for nagging him all of the time. Yeah, now it was all coming back, he told his wife that if she had been a better woman, perhaps he would be a better man. *What a horrible thing to say,* he thought to himself, but sadly it wasn't the only foolish thing he said. He was trying to hurt her feelings, even though deep down he knew the Bible commanded the husband to love his wife as he loved himself and to honor his wife as if she was a weaker vessel. Justine was strong, but too many years of his antics wore on her and the beautiful vibrant woman she had been when they first met had begun to lose her light. After birthing two children in the last five years and dealing with his shenanigans, who could blame her?

Jacob stood there and he remembered her telling him to leave. Why did he leave? He told his therapist it was because Justine hurt his feelings and he had been doing all he could to make her happy, but the truth came to him that night when he was sitting in his hotel room listening to Bishop T.D. Jakes on YouTube. The Bishop was speaking on manhood and He-Motions and then he felt something. A knowing in his Spirit that he hadn't felt in a long time. He went into the hotel bathroom that night and stared at himself in the mirror and that's when he confessed to himself, God, the angels, and any being that was listening that night, that he left because he knew she had been telling the truth about him and he wasn't ready to hear it or to change. Just then, he took a deep breath, saying to himself: *Remember your affirmation...where focus goes, energy flows. You can't undo the past, but you can focus on being a better you in the future.* Jacob stood there holding his luggage like holding a life raft, in that empty house decorated by his wife. How he missed her these last six months. He never wanted to be the kind of man who had to lose everything to realize how blessed he was. He started five years ago doing the total opposite. They had done things the "right" way, not having sex before marriage, going to counseling with the pastor of the church and praying together. The wedding was beautiful with them speaking vows that they wrote to one another. The first year was tough learning to live together, but they got through it, still praying together, and working through issues together. He would write her love notes every day and send flowers every week. Then the kids were born, Ethan, in year two of the marriage, and Erica in year four. After that, they seemed to argue and fight about everything. They started sleeping in separate rooms more and more and talking less and less. He even started working later at the office and going to the bar, just so he could avoid seeing her at night. This just made things worse because then she was upset with him because she felt like he was never there to help with the children, and she was right.

"What a fool I was, Doc," he said to his therapist in one of his sessions. As he reflected on these moments, he began to feel the weight of the luggage on his shoulders and in his hands, but he remained immobilized in the same spot. When he finally came to himself, he broke down and texted Justine. It was days before she responded, but those days were like a resuscitating machine, giving life back to what seemed to have been a dead soul. Then, when she agreed to meet him in a public place to talk, he was thanking God the entire drive to the little outdoor café they used to go to for lunches. Standing at the threshold, he recalled the look of indifference Justine gave him as he poured out his heart and apologized with desperation. He begged her to try marriage counseling. She admitted that their time apart almost broke her and that she was no longer in love with him, but she would try. Calling to mind the blank stare that she wore on her face, he was convinced in that moment that he had lost his wife, but he still went back to his room and prayed to God that her heart would change. He made a promise then that he would do whatever it took to work on himself and he did it. He tried different mindfulness activities including meditation (something he had never done before). The first session with the marriage counselor was hard. He had to listen to his wife recap all of the hurtful things that she internalized that because of his selfishness, he wasn't even aware of. In those sessions, he learned about physical ailments she had that she never told him about because she said, she didn't trust he would be supportive. What happened to him being priest, provider, and protector? "How did she even last five years," is what he asked his therapist in one of their later sessions. His friends tried to console him and tell him people make mistakes. Yes, they were right, people do make mistakes but Jacob knew better and he was determined to do better. He remembered the time he called the pastor and he told him the Scripture in Proverbs 24:16, F*or a righteous man falleth seven times, and riseth up again..."*

The night, he and Justine spoke on the phone, they prayed together one at a time, after which he told her he loved her. For the first time in months, she replied saying, "I love you too Jacob, but you really hurt me and I don't know if I can ever forget how you treated me, but I forgive you." It was the first time, she ever said that she forgave him or acknowledged his contrition. He wept that night as he thanked God for bringing them to that moment. He was in shock the next day when she texted him that he could come back home and that the kids missed him. After he asked her if she missed him and there was no response, he grinned, remembering the delayed text later that day that read, *Maybe, a little bit.* Standing there in the empty house, smelling the new furniture for the first time, holding the heavy luggage, he could no longer take it, and fell to his hands and knees praising God for allowing him another chance. As he rose from the semi-prostrate position, he could hear the garage door opening and the low rumble of Justine's SUV. Before that moment, it had been such a long time since the sound of her arrival invoked such a feeling of excitement. He heard the car doors slam and the side door next to the kitchen open and the familiar call of his children, "DADDY's home!" He looked up and saw the smile that he remembered from days that had seemed to fall into oblivion that he feared had been permanently erased and then he remembered two scriptures he had read: Hosea 6:1, *Come let us return to the Lord, He has torn us to pieces but he will heal us: he has injured us but he will bind up our wounds* and Isaiah 61:7, *Instead of your shame you will receive a double portion, and instead of disgrace you will rejoice in your inheritance. And so you will inherit a double portion in your land, and everlasting joy will be yours.*

Jacob had fallen, but now he was restored.

Selah

Email: sjbookstores@gmail.com

Website: https://sj-bookstores.square.site

Social Media - http://www.facebook.com/steven5674; www.facebook.com/sjbookstores

Achievement to Success by God's Way
By Angela McClain

Believe. Believe in your success. Believe in you. Believe God.

In seeking success, where do you often find yourself? What goals do you have in place to progress forward? You long to be someone of significance in the world. With a common goal, you can. The common goal is going for what God has called you to be. You are meant to be successful. Here is the reason. You were chosen by God to become who He created you to be.

When you dream, God will show you His vision He assigned to you. Stay on the path of obedience to do God's work He assigned to you. God has a plan and purpose for your life. If you are not sure of direction in your life, pray, seek, and ask God to reveal your purpose. He will reveal His purpose to you. Every step you take towards your goals and dreams leads you closer to your success.

Don't give up on pursuing your goals and dreams. Don't allow distractions keep you from pursuing your goals and dreams. Continue to pursue your goals and dreams. Those small steps towards your goals and dreams can turn into big accomplishments. God does not want you to give up on His purpose. Don't think that you are a success. With God's help and encouragement, know and claim you are a success.

Prayer for Inspiration in Success

Dear Father God: Thank You for Your goodness and many blessings. Thank You for Your faithfulness to navigate and guide us through. Thank you, for being the lifter of our heads, when low feelings overwhelm us. Thank You for Your Word which comforts and reminds us of Your promises and purpose for our lives. Thank You for taking away our doubts, fears, and worries, and reminding us to rely fully on You. In Jesus' Name. Amen.

Thankful for God's Gifts

Lord, we thank You, for the gifts, as we commit to use them in Your Honor. Anoint our projects, goals, dreams, for each accomplishment may bring You glory. With Your light, may our work bring faith, joy, and a smile to many. In Jesus' Name. Amen.

Prayer for Success

My heart's desire is to be obedient in pursuit of Your Will for my life, and to abound in the good works You've created me to do. I ask You to lead and guide me on the path to success, to progress the advancement of Your Kingdom. As I put you first in everything I do, I embrace Your many blessings. In Jesus' Name. Amen.

Psalm 90:17

And let the beauty of the LORD our God be upon us: and establish thou the work of our hands upon us; yea, the work of our hands establish thou it.

Email: amediting35@gmail.com

Shake The fear

By Kent Wade

Small Voice (SV): "Take a deep breath Kent Wade and let it out of your nose slowly."

Kent Wade: *Breathes deeply and exhales slowly. "I have walked into this building a thousand times!"

SV: "Then why are you so nervous?"

Kent: "Come on now!!! You know why...!"

SV: "So you are afraid of growing up?"

Kent: "I am afraid that I might not be ready to take this leap."

SV: "Well, it's too late to back out now. Don't forget the reason why you are here."

Kent: "I know. It's time to shake this fear."

Eight months before this 'mirror talk,' a conversation between humans and the small voice inside of our heads, I was an employee of the Kankakee Public Library. Even before January 5, 2005, I was a teenager pulling open the doors to the central station of my city. So walking through the front doors was literally like stepping into my home. More so, during the times when I was actually homeless. Come to think about it, I have grown in ALMOST every capacity there is to experience via the library, even performing janitorial duties.

It felt comfortable... It felt right... It was as natural as breathing. But that was eight months ago.

That was when I saw my LIFE being tied to a fear. There was a belief that if I just followed a 'certain' path I would reach my ultimate goal. My fear always sat screaming at me in the rearview whenever the journey was going off road. How could I leave my first real job as an adult? Why would I stop working with teens without a strong support system? Who could turn down the free food that co-workers brought from home?! Does it look good to turn your back on the people who helped you learn to believe in you?? So to avoid answering those questions, it was best to stay the course, even if I was miserable.

Merriam- Webster Dictionary defines fear as, an unpleasant, often strong, emotion caused by anticipation or danger. Meaning that fear is present when we perceive that we are in danger or have cause for excitement during waiting. This powerful feeling or perception can be compared to a sandbag. At first, it begins as a thought when we are faced with a new idea but it does not stop the flow. Eventually, when visited enough, that idea can be like hundreds of sandbags stopping the course of a stream. As fear grows it controls. As it is entertained, fear will create false realities that support staying 'safe.'

Safe was no longer an option as my 'mirror talk' concluded. After another deep breath, my attention shifted to me turning on an iTunes playlist entitled, "Let's Work." With Big K.R.I.T filling my ears with bass and words of inspiration, I pulled open the doors of my former employer, focused on finishing the mission started eight months ago. That mission was to begin shaking the fear.

Shaking fear is easier said than done.

Shaking fear involves three vital elements. Each element is a piece that connects to another, thus working with one another to bring out results of awesome proportions. First, acknowledging that there is fear to begin with. We all want to appear like we are tougher than dry skin on a cold day, but we have to be honest. It's liberating to be honest. We ALL have had a moment where we experience an unpleasant emotion caused by anticipation or danger! Doesn't it feel better to let that out and know that someone else can relate? Seeing that there is a problem is vital in addressing that problem. My patience had run out for waiting for the right time to do more with my abilities. Next, deciding whether the fear is a danger or anticipation provides clear focus for action. When in danger, fight or flight kicks in automatically. Danger means that one's life is in jeopardy. We confuse danger with anticipation of, "What if...?" I questioned my worth, my loyalty, and even my own purpose because there was no clear map as to what will happen. Heck, I didn't even know what I was doing. But when properly analyzed, we can prepare our action plan. Lastly, once we have assessed and prepared our plan, we must take the leap. The heart will be pounding. Palms will be sweaty. Knees will be weak. Words will fumble. Just leap. Moving forward is the biggest step to shaking the fear, next to admitting it's there.

The leap for me was resigning from the library. There was the desire to control the narrative of how I impacted the world. Next, I begin to focus solely on building my public speaking services, which I was doing part-time for five years, working on the foundation and reaching out to former clients, working tirelessly to share with the world that I was ready to speak full time!! Filled with purpose and hunger, I begin using my free time to learn more and to meet new people. After the leap of leaving the library, there was this fuel to take more leaps! Nothing was off the table, but it had to align with my mission and doing it my way. The fear was being shaken.

Even after fear has been shaken, it does not mean it is gone. It is like washing your face. You have to do it daily to ensure you are clean. Walking through the building after leaving, it was surreal. I never imagined a world where I didn't work at the KPL. Climbing the stairs felt like climbing the stairway to Heaven. There was a brief pause in time as I entered a conference room on the third floor that I have sweated in preparing for professionals who rented it out for years. Tears begin to fill my eyes as participants for my first ever workshop arrived. After choking back those same tears, there is a rush in my veins as I introduce myself;

Kent: "My name is Kent Wade. I am a professional speaker, host, and facilitator. I am a husband and father of four. I am also proud to share that I am the first Black to be elected as an officer of the Board of Directors of the very library we are meeting in. Might I add that I worked here for twelve years and was an active teen patron. So who is ready to SHAKE THE FEAR!

SV: "My boy is all grown up. Now give them every dose of ambition that you got!"

iamkentwade.com

Nah Son

By Shawn Robinson

Most people are probably expecting me to give a bunch of tips about how to properly brand and market yourself, but I'm going to take a different approach. I hold many titles, Child of God, Man, Son, Pastor, Designer, Consultant, Creative Director, and probably about five more, but the most important and usually negotiated is Shawn. We walk around looking to be everyone's everything, but end up losing ourselves in the process. When a friend or family member is in trouble we're so quick to pick up a cape and try to rescue them, without thought or care of our own condition. We work for smiles and laughter, but inside we search for someone that will bring those things that we seek out.

SO why am I saying all this? Is this a come to Jesus moment? Is this an opportunity for me to vent? Or is it a chance to come clean, in the hopes that these couple of pages will help someone else avoid the pitfalls of self-denial?

Self-Denial is the denial of one's own interests and needs; self-sacrifice. (Definition provided by Oxford Dictionary)

When it comes to your relationship with God, make sure you place Him first and let Him transform the desires of your heart. Take delight in the LORD, and he will give you the desires of your heart, Psalms 37:4. So many times we treat happiness as a carnival game prize. We spend everything to get it and once we do, it's a fleeting feeling. What we should be in search of is Joy. That joy from the Lord which can't be taken away. I've searched and searched for people, things, and jobs to fulfill areas that they had no true ability to fill. They could only be filled by a Higher Power. Growing up as an only child, you learned to do everything on your own. So you build a sense of selfishness as a defense mechanism. If I only look out for myself, then I can't be disappointed. You build a I, Me, and Self mentality.

So you're wondering how you can give of yourself so freely in the first paragraph, but call yourself selfish in the paragraph above. It's because your desire is to bring happiness to others to help you smile. When you do for others, it's for self-glory, verses purity of intent. Now it's not to say that you're not doing it to help that person, but what's your real motive?

Also love, LOVE. It's nothing better than that feeling of telling someone you love them and they say it back. Or those butterflies and constant thoughts of the person. Wanting to spend endless amounts of time just talking about nothing. Then it begins to wear off and you wonder if it was really love or another lustful adventure. If it is love, then why does it not operate in the guidelines of my expectations? Why does it take work? Isn't everyday supposed to be smiles and kisses? Nah, son! So, I dated and dated and dated (Long-term) and was even married. But without the true image or definition of love I ended up leaving a trail of broken hearts and painful regrets. I leaned on immaturity and foolishness. What the heck is communication? Promises of future communication was just the ability to hold off the conservation till next time. So what did I learn? Love is defined by first looking at how God loves us, unconditionally. Without want! Without quitting because someone disappointed you. Love from God is unmeasurable and thank Him for that. Because if God acted in the way that I did, well let's just say, "Oh boy!" But He doesn't and He didn't. Thank God for Mercy! I would like to take this time to apologize to all those women that I hurt, because I wasn't ready to use the words I spoke to you. I apologize for any pain it brought you and the mental space that it took up. All I can say is that with now understanding that Love is a choice, I will choose wisely when and how to use it, so that no one else is impacted. Oh yeah, one of the biggest components has been learning to love me. Truly, love me, not the fake Shawn I put on to make others happy, but the goofy, nerd that loves comic book movies and technology.

When you establish a relationship with God it allows you to truly state, "I can." But followed by, "Do all things through Christ who strengthens me." I wore this necklace that said that for about a year or so to remind me daily of that. Whenever I get overwhelmed or begin to overthink, it gives me encouragement and the willingness to fight. I wish I could say that I look to that Scripture every time, sometimes I choose to wallow in self-pity, I lean onto MY own understanding. I turned mole holes into mountains, all within my head. I defeated myself even before attempting to enter into some battles. But when you get tired of the constant mental fight, you either fight or take flight. And this isn't an energy drink, so I had to learn how to fight. I originally thought that the fight was physical, that I could work my way through my problems. Again, nah, son! Why do you fight a battle that isn't meant for you to fight? If you have the greatest warrior of all time having your back, then why do you keep standing against the wall? Free! Do you trust Him? This battle is spiritual first, then natural. Until I realized this, I was wondering and pondering about solutions to my own problems and I had a cheat sheet around me all the time. It gets to the point where you decide, for God I live and for God I die or is it? I do what I want and maybe when I die, I'll be at peace. Nope, it doesn't work like that. God wants that relationship and for so long I told myself that my relations with God was sufficient; but yet, I was studying and learning on a level I wasn't meant to be on. Meaning an 18-year-old, shouldn't be reading books meant for a preschooler. God wants to take you to new heights in Him, are you ready to sacrifice and do the Godly work to get there? If you do that, you will live a truly blessed life.

So, YOU CAN overcome anything! Find you a great Spiritual Covering, Mine is Be Whole Christian Center and my Apostle and Prophetess equip you with the tools you need to be free indeed. Read your Word daily. Pray, Fast and must importantly don't be afraid to use that 13-letter word COMMUNICATION. BE Blessed and continue working toward being whole.

Info@727marketingllc.com
www.727marketingllc.com

A Masterpiece

By Yolanda E. Brown

Have you ever been in a season of your life where it seems like you are on track and things are going well, yet still feel like you do not know who you are? Yeah, me too! I was in that very same place. You can be thriving in business, making all kinds of connections, traveling around the world, standing on stages, and being in rooms with millionaires, yet still question yourself. Can I be honest with you? I have been there too. You have people who admire things about you, things you are liked for, things that were even spoken into your life. However, in reality none of that really matters when you do not know who you truly are from the inside. Regardless of what great compliments you receive, you still began to question yourself. We cause a lot of damage to ourselves mentally and emotionally when we question ourselves. You begin to look for things in places you know that are not going to provide the answer. You start to tap into the wrong sources for temporary comfort. You start doubting that you truly know who you are, where you belong, and that you are okay.

This may sound crazy, but I have learned that the most challenging, life-changing, and thought-provoking question is and will always be, "Who Are You?" Why is that? Because when you begin to doubt and question everything about you and why you are in certain places, then it is time to look at the core of your heart. This was my breaking point. Here began the challenge and then the life change. For the first time, I had to really face myself and deal with who I was and how I saw myself then dive into who God is and what He says I am to counter all the things that were keeping me in a bound or stagnant place. So, I sat and prayed that God would begin to reveal the real me to me. As time went on, God began to show me things that I said, and the things that I was holding to that was keeping me from not only moving forward, but also the things that were not allowing room for our relationship to develop and become natural. He instructed that I needed to get to know Him better than I would come to know me. *But why*? Because on the surface, NO, rather on appearance and paper it looked like I knew who I was, where I was headed, what I was doing, and I was close to Him (so I thought). I was succeeding in areas of my life, but failing at my very core. I remember praying before I went to bed to wake up pouring my heart out. At 3:30 early one Thursday morning I sat broken in tears for two hours with God saying, create in me a clean heart and renew a right spirit within me, I am tired of not knowing who I am and feeling defeated and undeserving. I cried those words over and over with great expectation of change each time I said them. God knew everything about me, and nothing was hidden. Watch this, the difference this time was my heart's posture.

God wanted to hear it from the depth of my heart and out of my mouth. I was open about every hurt, every mistake, every thought (right or wrong), every reason why I felt I was not enough or worthy, everything I did not like about myself, the very struggles I carried from suicidal thoughts, to pornography, being in a relationship with a recovering addict that I would later become an enabler to, compromising to please someone else's needs, being a minister who had a baby out of wedlock, and focusing on the love I was not receiving instead of being grateful for the love I had and was still experiencing. All those things made me question who I was. Once I had released all that to God, He began to break the strongholds. His words became clearer and rang in my heart. I could see my mind becoming clearer from all that mess. My heart was free to make room for God's love, peace, joy, and promises. I started to speak life daily over myself. Even when something tries to creep in, I stop right there and speak positive thoughts. I am the head and not the tail. I lack nothing in God's hands, I am the apple of His eye. I am fearfully and wonderfully made. God made no mistakes when He formed me in my mother's womb. My mistakes are my testimony and God's glory, and so on. I get up and go to bed every day with thanksgiving, praise, and worship on my lips because it was nobody but God who could have changed me. Most importantly, my life Scripture (I made it personal) became Ephesians 2:10, which is also the reason for my nonprofit, "For I am (we are) God's masterpiece (handiwork) created (anew) in Christ Jesus, so we can do the good works he planned for me (us) to do." So yes, I am worthy, I am loved, I am enough, I belong, and I am chosen and qualified to be in certain places because God created me for them and opened the doors for me to walk in, no matter who thinks I am qualified or not. I am everything God says I am. Once I got that in my spirit, and truly received and believed it, I walk with my head up and in the fullness of the masterpiece that I was created to be.

If this is you, I ask you to just think about who you are for just a moment. Then answer the question, "Who are you?" And if you have questioned yourself, doubted yourself, or just do not know how to see yourself, take this time to get the real answers you are looking for. Because the things we are associated with, where we live, what we do, or what we make is just a small fraction of who we are, but it is not who we are at the core. You may say well that was you. And you are right, it was me. However, the same God that did it for me is the same God that is waiting for you, and will do it for you as well. You are not in this alone. I am here, cheering you on and praying for you to get to know the real you through the eyes of God. Because yes you too are deserving to be in places no one thinks is for you. You belong. You are worthy. You are equipped to great works. You are enough. Now you ask, "How do I navigate through this to get the answers?" First, of all, be completely honest with yourself and God. Which means peeling layers back that you have covered up very well and that have become your stumbling block or hindrance in moving forward which has caused you to doubt who you are. Secondly, you have to seek God, get in your Word, and ask for God to show you the real you through His eyes and words. There is nothing God does not know about you already that you would like to believe is hidden from Him. He is waiting on you to love you and blow your mind with all the goodness He has designed and created within you in mind. Next, be intentional about your relationship with Him and your heart's posture. And watch your life begin to transform in front of you. Finally, take everything that you thought and throw it out by replacing it with what God says. The process is not, but if you are honest, it is so worth it. Know that your life will be forever changed so that you can walk in the fullness of the masterpiece that God created you to be. There is a quote that is fitting for this, it says:

"You were handpicked by God. You are LOVED. You are a person of extreme value and significance. You are a MASTERPIECE." ~Unknown

Know that you know You Are ONE of a KIND! If you take away one thing, I pray you take this: As you tap into who you are, walk with your head up and with confidence because you are UNSTOPPABLE in the very essence of who you are and were created to be.

Website: www.created4goodworks.com
Email: yolandabrnpa@gmail.com

Part 2 - YOU CAN HEAL, FORGIVE & OVERCOME

You Are Enough

By Lorriell Lockhart

"Your greatest responsibility is to love yourself and know you are enough!"

I was bullied so much in my life from grammar school all the way to high school. I believed all the lies told to me: "You're fat and ugly." I was deemed unlikable not by the character of my heart, but because I looked different from other kids. This was hard to process, especially being so young. I spent all of grammar school trying to stay out of the spotlight. My only thought was: *They can't ridicule you if they forget you're around.* This followed me all the way to high school, and I know what some of you are thinking*: Lorriell, why didn't you tell or stand up for yourself? I'm sure they would have left you alone.* Trust me, I tried everything! It only made it worse. I stood up for myself, and I would get in trouble. I would yell, cry, and cause a scene. No one could see me drowning, so the bullying just got worse.

I'm not telling you this so you can feel pity for me, but I'm telling you this so you can learn how I overcame, and you can too!

Fast forward to the day I finally had enough with bullying and decided it wasn't going to control my life anymore. It was a regular day of high school, but it seemed like there was a target on my back, and everybody had a perfect aim that day. I was being attacked by everyone for no reason. When I got out of school, I was exhausted emotionally and mentally. I had enough when I got home. I went to my room and stood in the mirror, listing off every so-called flaw they said I had. "You're fat." You're ugly." "You're not cool enough." "You don't wear name brand."

I began to cry. I could only see what they labeled me as and not who I actually was. That day I started speaking over myself daily, replacing things like: *you're fat* to *I was made perfectly in God's image,* or *you're ugly* into: *beauty is in the eye of the beholder,* and to me: *I am beautiful!* I began to speak affirmations over myself, things like: *I am bold. I am confident. I am enough. I am loved. I am okay with just being me and not who they want me to be.* It took me meeting myself and falling in love with the girl I met instead of hating the image of her that they made.

My last words to you are: Yeah bullies have power, but not as much power as self-love holds. You have to learn how to be so comfortable with being yourself that others have no choice but to follow suit. never believe the lies they tell you. Your beauty and light deserve to exist in the world unapologetically. You deserve to love yourself unconditionally. You deserve to have joy that doesn't waver because of others' opinion. You deserve nights free of crying because they made you hate yourself. You deserve to confidently smile in pictures and not feel self-conscious. You deserve the world even if it means giving it to yourself. You are more incredible than you know, and you deserve more than you think. Know your worth and NEVER SETTLE FOR LESS THAN YOU DESERVE! If I can do, it you can too!

lorrielllockhart10@gmail.com

A Sassy Cancer Survivor: My Journey

By Janae Anderson

I am a sassy, strong survivor, overcomer, warrior, thriver, and this is my story of my cancer journey. Have you ever thought to yourself how strong you really are? If you asked me 10 years ago where I would be now, I would have never thought I would be here to tell you. On May 14, 2010 I was given the worst news a 22-year college student could have asked for, I was diagnosed with Acute Lymphoblastic Leukemia. Leading up to this diagnosis, I was very ill and had been seeking answers for a year. I had many long road trips to different cities to see specialists and many emergency room visits, which none of them gave me the answers I was hoping for. At this point, I never gave up on how I was feeling and knew in my gut there was something wrong, but no one would listen to me.

Since I was a young woman, they would always say, "You are too young to have cancer and to have any serious health problems." I remember the doctors would tell me it was anxiety and it was all in my head and to not worry. What was giving me anxiety was the fact the doctors were not listening to me, and soon enough I would end up six feet under. At one point in my journey to figuring out what was wrong, I ended up having the police show up to my house because I had threatened to kill myself because I was so done with everyone not caring anymore. Well after that, I ended up at the hospital once again, and all I remember was being sedated and having to see a counselor. After that, I decided I shouldn't listen to my gut instinct anymore and gave in to what the doctors were saying. It was not much longer, when I was writing my final English paper when I felt lumps in my neck and in my armpits. The next morning, I woke up with odd-looking bruises on the insides of my arms. It was the last day of my semester and I had to go to school, but my mom decided to call the doctor's office and get me in to be seen.

I ended up going to school and had turned in my final paper and I could barely breathe to get to my mom's car. I had to sit down in the grass and called her and she said, "We're going to the doctor right away." Once again, I was faced with the fear of being sent home because they would say it's just another Urinary Tract Infection. However, I overcame the fear and I went in and they said what I thought they would say. They weren't going to run any blood work, until my mother decided to step in and say, "No, you are going to run blood work on her." I could not believe my eyes; they saw all these red and purple bruises down my arm and lumps in my throat and they weren't going to do anything. Well I am glad my mom took over and made them do it.

Later that night I should say, we received a phone call from my primary care doctor asking me weird questions and not sharing the results with us. The main one I remember the most was, "Do you have a boyfriend, and have he abused you? I then replied, "No, why?" What made me really upset was he knew the results and it felt like he is making a joke out of this. Then he proceeded to say, I need you to go to the emergency room immediately because your platelets are down to 13,000. The normal range for platelets is anywhere from 200,000-400,000. At that time, I was unaware of what was happening and ended up waiting in the emergency room for eight hours until I was admitted onto the Oncology Unit. They had given me my first set of platelets, what would have been my first of 30 or more. At this time, I knew God had my back that night because the ER doctor was someone my mom new from her business. I met her days before I ended up in the ER, it was a blessing in disguise.

As I was willed into the Oncology Unit, we had no clue of what was going on with me. It wasn't until the next day where my parents and I got to meet with an oncologist. The doctor's name was Dr Reddy, he explained to us of how we needed to do a bone marrow biopsy to see what is happening in my marrow. According to the doctor, my white blood count was extremely elevated alongside with my platelets being low; therefore, there was something wrong. We ended up doing the bone marrow biopsy and boy, did it hurt. The pain was worth finding out what was wrong with me, but I had no clue what was going to happen. It was not until five days later when I was told I had cancer and I only had two weeks to live.

After finding out I had only two weeks to live, the doctor gave me no option but to start chemotherapy the next day. How does someone handle such devastating news and panic? A positive attitude and great support system were two of the biggest factors into my recovery. I was heartbroken but at the same time I was ready to begin this journey to being cancer free. Yes, cancer is horrible, but I finally had a diagnosis they could help me recover from. After many months of searching, we had been given answers and I could either choose to not fight or give it the best fight of my life. Of course, I decided to fight for my life even knowing how hard the battle is about to be. Having a great support system and knowing I would be taken good care and knowing God has a plan for me, made it an easier fight. It was not too long before starting chemotherapy, the doctor explained how long my treatment and what types of chemotherapy I would be receiving. He went into detail and said for a year, I would receive inpatient chemo for one week out of every month, and then be able to go home and go to the outpatient center to receive all the blood and platelet transfusions.

My one-week chemo included a different type each day, leading up to a 24-hour chemotherapy on Friday, all these drugs would lower my immune system to zero and I could not fight any infections. In treatment, I was told when my counts are low, I had to social distance and isolate myself from the world. By having to isolate myself, it made people seem to get scared, and I felt they were nervous to be around me. Have you ever felt like you were alone when there were many people around you? At the beginning of my diagnosis, a lot of my friends showed up to my room and it was awesome. However, once I got further down the road, it felt like I was losing friends.

After a year, I would be doing two and half years of additional chemo which would consist of oral treatment every day and once a week infusion of chemo. He also explained how I would be getting power port inside my chest and a **peripherally inserted central catheter** (PICC) line in my arm. This was all very overwhelming, and I was being told to take it one day at a time. I was lucky to have a nurse who was my designated coach to help me get through my challenges. Throughout this process, I learned how much strength I had. Even on my weakest days, I had no idea how strong my body was. I was in the hospital for a total of 30 days until they let me go home until my next round of chemotherapy.

Going through this process of all the unknowns was terrifying, and losing my hair and gaining 60 pounds was hard for me to handle. It was all worth it when four months had passed, and the doctor gave us the good news of how my chemotherapy had been working and there are no signs of cancer anywhere in my body. Yet, I still had to do my full length of chemo so the cancer wouldn't come back. After seven years being of chemo it has not yet come back.

As I am typing this, we have about four days until my 10-year diagnoses date, and it's to this day, hard to believe I overcome cancer. It has taken me many years of therapy and guidance to get where I am today. Not only did I kick cancer in the butt, I have been able to graduate with honors and I am going to get married. It has been no easy journey to get to this point, life has thrown me many curveballs, but cancer has taught me that I can overcome anything I want to. Cancer has taught me to face my fears and just try to live one day at a time. I am grateful to be able to share my story to everyone around the world, and this isn't even half of it. What I want to tell people is cancer doesn't define me, but it sure has made me become the person I am today. Cancer has showed me the strength I have never knew I had before, it has taught me to speak up for myself. I have a voice, and I am capable of sharing my story.

ilove2smile07@gmail.com

You Can Be Free!
TRUE LIBERTY— FREEDOM
By Nicole L. Walker

2020 daily headlines run the gamut globally with topics ranging from pandemic, Coronavirus, COVID-19, shelter in, lockdowns, antibodies, vaccines, deaths, and recoveries. With all the topics, the focus is centered on freedom. Around the world people are desperate to break free, to be loosed from the bondage that is pestilence, disease and economic woes. People are ready to exit their homes in defiance and rebellion against newly implemented measures that if adhered to, could ensure the safety and health of many. As a two-time COVID-19 survivor, I can attest that you can have the freedom you have need of, but not necessarily the kind you desire. I have access to this freedom and YOU CAN too!

Mostly people are looking to be released physically from restrictions and a bondage that was imposed on them because of unforeseen circumstances: Global Pandemic. Along with these physical limits are the psychological constraints brought on by the same pesky culprit. There is a remedy. It is a once and for all, end all, liberating power. This gift was afforded to us by Christ when He paid the ultimate cost with His life. Though you may not have been looking for it specifically while looking for a simplistic freedom from physical and mental bondage you have stumbled upon the ultimate FREEDOM; from sin and the penalty of sin. This freedom is all encompassing.

Stand fast therefore in the liberty by which Christ has made us free, and do not be entangled again with a yoke of bondage. Galatians 5:1 NKJV

According to this scripture, we are to stand firm and not be bound, because it is through His own freedom Christ has freed us. The freedom of Christ is completely liberating. Not only are we free from sin, the penalty of sin which is death but free in all aspects of our lives. The sacrifice of Christ allows us to be free even in the midst of a disease or death.

We are admonished to not be entangled again with the yoke of bondage. When we are freed by Christ it is once and for all except we forfeit our freedom by relinquishing it to someone or succumbing to our circumstances. This freedom was freely given to us and should not just be given away. It is ours to keep. Once received, it is imperative to not go back into bondage, not turn back to our sinful nature. We are to not become entangled again because it is possible for us to subject ourselves to something worse.

"Afterward Jesus found him in the temple, and said to him, "See, you have been made well. Sin no more, lest a worse thing come upon you." John 5:14 NKJV

The freedom of Christ allows us to be free in our minds, in our spirit, in our health and even with our bodies. With the freedom of Christ there are no limits by which we can be bound. This liberty, though it is completely liberating does come with warning;

"I have the right to do anything," you say--but not everything is beneficial. "I have the right to do anything"--but not everything is constructive. 1 Corinthians 10:23 NIV

True liberty, true freedom is not doing what you want to because you can. It is not doing what you feel like doing because you can. True freedom is having the right to do anything, but only doing what you should and not doing as you please. Even though you are able to do anything because you are free, all of those things may not be edifying to self or beneficial to self or others. Freedom should not be abused.

Oftentimes you hear prisoners say that they are not prisoners but instead they are free. These prisoners have tapped into something. They have freed themselves in their minds. Note that except you know Jesus, the Word of God and abide in the Word of God then it is impossible to truly be free.

"Then Jesus said to those Jews who believed Him, "If you abide in My Word, you are My disciples indeed. And you shall know the truth, and the truth shall make you free."

John 8:31-32 NKJV

1. NO FREEDOM without Jesus
2. NO FREEDOM without the WORD
3. NO FREEDOM if you do not ABIDE in the WORD

Abide, continue, dwell, endure, be present, remain, stand, and tarry

In many circles, we usually hear only verse 32 of John 8 but verse 31 is where the power lies. True freedom comes from relationship with Jesus Christ. Freedom was given to us by God through Christ. We are able to be free because we are joint-heirs with Christ. We must abide in and the Word of God must dwell in us. We must know and use the Word of God because the Word unlocks the truth. What is this truth? The truth is Jesus, the testimony of Jesus. It is by knowing this truth that we are made free. The truth of Jesus Christ liberates us. Adhering to the above scripture ensures the ability to have and maintain freedom.

We have seen many looking to break free. Where there is freedom there is always some form rebellion. With coronavirus we have those rebelling against, being sheltered in, against wearing masks, those against the closing of businesses and now those against government. I am a witness in these times that no sickness, pestilence, disease, shackle of the body or mind is able hold you bound if you have the freedom of Christ. I have the freedom of Christ. The sickness could not hold me. A long recovery could not hold me. Walking through the shadow of death with my family could not hold me. Fear could not grip me. Possible lost wages could not render me bound. I am not even bound by being quarantined. It is not because I am special or think more highly of myself than I ought. It is because I have found the truth. The truth of Jesus Christ has been revealed to me. The knowledge of the truth has made me free. Jesus Christ has made me free. Freedom is mine. I will not relinquish or forfeit my freedom. It will be maintained through relationship with Christ and abiding in the Word of God. I will not be denied. I have freedom. YOU CAN TOO!

Therefore if the Son makes you free, you shall be free indeed."
John 8:36 NKJV

Kingdomperspective2020@gmail.com

My Pain Had Become Part of My Purpose to Inspire Others

By Colette Mobley

At a young age, I used to dream about all the things I wanted to do when I became grown. I had no idea of the things I would become a part of, the places I would travel, nor the storms I would live through. When you grow up, you never imagine the life you will encounter. At the age of five, I had a mentality where I was so serious about life and the direction I knew I wanted to travel. I found myself daydreaming about my life, but didn't know how life and others would treat me. I would write things down to be able to remind me of what I wanted to encounter. Watching the things that my mom endured, remembering her pain, her struggles of raising a black child alone, her broken heartedness mixed with depression was real every day in my life. Even from that age, my mom had no idea of how much I mirrored her life into my own. I admired her for her strength, courage, wisdom, love of others, and the sacrifices she made to help others.

As I began to live after suffering from sexual abuse, depression, and even trying to commit suicide at the tender age of five, I spent my life hiding my inner disturbances. My parents were no longer together as I was growing up after their abusive marriage and I would visit them at my leisure, although I lived with my mother. I began to see how their strengths and weaknesses made a difference in how I began to see myself. I kept writing about the day that I would meet my knight in shining armor, but when I got older, I learned life was so much more different than just daydreams and fairytales. As I grew older, I began to really see life for how it is, or at least so I thought. I kept trying to put myself in protective mode because my mom kept me away from everything or everybody. But little did she know the damage was happening to her youngest child. I was put right amid those she thought where I would be safe, but only to put me in harm's way. My mother left me with her boyfriends' family which who had molested me. I slid deeper into loneliness, sorry, and more heartaches. At that precious age, I kept trying to talk to her, share what was going on, but she was too busy in her own world of pain and partying life to drink it away. Things that were happening to me, didn't stop at my younger years, I didn't have many friends and my mom wouldn't let others come to visit me nor could I go to their homes without my mom visiting the parents.

I kept praying, and even at a young age, attending church to try to keep myself focused on the right path. I learned about who I was and how I can overcome the rough times in my life. I began to get involved with other activities at church and in school, trying to be around others I thought were like me. I was often picked on and talked about because I never fit in with others. As I got older, I began to become more involved with church, ministry, reading my Bible, and talking to other family members. I didn't know it, but my foundation of my painful past was leading me to help others who were going through the same things that I had just survived. It began to lead me in the right direction of a greater person that I was becoming and into a greater woman on today. I then met others who was like me and we shared our stories at other events that will help others to get help and be encouraged from us sharing what we did. It was not easy to share the stories of such pain, but it still worked out for my good in the end.

There were so many times that I wanted to give up, I wanted to give in, throw in the towel, but I know I had to continue to fight to inspire and be encouraging. I had to tell myself that there is a greater reason, a greater focus, and a lesson with a great purpose for me. I speak to others to let them know we all have valuable gifts that have been placed inside of us, and it is up to us to share it with others. There are so many people whom I have met along the way in me sharing my life stories, my tribulations and most of all how I still made it out of where I came from. From looking at me, you would have never guessed that I have come from such situations. It is always easier to look at a pretty picture and think: *I bet you that she has not had a rough life.* But if you ask the person, you can surely know and learn differently.

I used to be angry about my struggles and falls in the road, but they all have taught me to never give up; never stop sharing what you have with others so that they will stay encouraged to never give up. If I made it, I know you can as well. Don't be afraid to share what you have gone through; you would be surprised at whose life can be changed just from you sharing what you have gone through. Too many of us have even said what we will do in a certain situation, but we truly have no idea if the right pressures were to be applied to our lives. I said some things years ago that I never thought I would have to endure, then I went through and had to eat what I shared. I hope what I shared will inspire you to inspire others to help someone on today.

CoaTheAuthor2020@hotmail.com

708-307-1626

Truth Hurts, But God Heals

By Jasmine Nicole

Truth hurts. God heals and restores. When I finally decided to let go of my past, everything I experienced, all the trials and tribulations I've encountered in the last nineteen years (I'm twenty now) of my life to finally get healing from it. I had to realize some things. I've been hurt and others hurt me, but I did wrong to other people, too. I hurt others, too. How? You may ask me. I hurt the person who loves me more than life, who knew me before I was created in my mother's womb. I am fearfully and wonderfully made in His image, which was my heavenly Father. I hurt Him because I basically told Him that His love was not good enough, but I felt, for me to receive love, I had to look for it in people. I spent time looking for my Father when He was in my face all along.

He was trying to get my attention, and I turned my back on Him. I allowed people in my life, and He warned me not to, a lot of things I could have avoided, but I was being hardheaded. I was ashamed of myself that I lost sight of who He created me to be. Which is the salt to the earth, the light. Instead, I was ashamed, and what I wanted, I felt like everyone around me was, and that I was too young.

I remember I went to go see this visual sermon put on by Pastor Steve Munsey, and it was, *The White Throne Judgement,* and the sermon was basically about when we come to face judgement and just, the story line of the individuals who went up before God, regular people, even some celebrities made me realize I don't have time, and I honestly cannot be ashamed of Jesus anymore, because if I continued to deny Him before man, He would deny me before His Father. And I do want eternal life and I want to be happy. But if I keep pushing my heavenly Father away, I will never feel whole. I hurt my mother because all she did was be there for me, and I pushed her away because I was so hurt. I was mad at her with why she chose my father instead of any other man, and I felt like she never understood me, and she was holding me back, but I know she was protecting me from running wild, there is no telling what would've happened if she would've let me just spiral out of control. I hurt my brothers by being mean to them, my grandmother, my church family, and even other guys, because I was busy trying to use them to fill that loneliness. I would use other people knowing I really didn't like them, and I was using them to make myself feel better about myself when they didn't even do anything, but it made me feel even worse.

All my life, I was living, trying to be someone I wasn't. When I decided, no more. I had no clue who I was. I pretended for so long, I didn't know how to be myself. I held on to my trust issues, which was hard for me to really be myself with people. I was so tired of being mistreated and people stepping on my heart. I thought if I became coldhearted, it would teach people a lesson and if they thought they knew me they were dead wrong. I didn't even realize I had so much anger that I had pent-up inside of me that it was rage and I was just exploding on everything and everyone in my way. But at the end of the day I was also hurting because I was hurting people I cared about, but I just wanted to be selfish, and wanted to carry on my own mess, but it was no good for me. I had lost all motivation and was going to give up my dreams because I felt at one point that I didn't have purpose.

This healing process was not an easy one because this time things I haven't even thought that happened many years ago had surfaced. Things I chose to ignore and bury came back in my face and this time I couldn't run from them. I had to face them and take them head on. It was uncomfortable, and had me thinking, and I laughed at a lot of those things because I realized how silly and foolish I was, I literally thought I was in love the last four years of high school. Some memories I cringed, hating that even happened. With everything that has happened to me, I no longer held any regrets, and I was able to forgive those people and most importantly forgive myself.

AJNJaz1821@gmail.com

You Can Let Go

By Jessica Loper

10:00 A.M. Memorial Day, 2011...

Hungover.

Miserable.

Lonely.

Depressed.

Again.

I didn't want to get out of bed, but enough was enough. I was finally ready to accept and admit that I had a problem with alcohol. I had spent five years stuck in a vicious cycle. It was time to get out. I'd been ignoring that little voice inside me for long enough, the one that had been saying, "Give up alcohol and your life will change."

I had been living my life on autopilot, secretly drinking more than anybody around me. I'd get home from work each day, head straight to my closet, for my welcome home vodka shot, even before setting my purse down. After setting my things down, I'd mix up a second drink to take with me in the shower. I'd spend the rest of my night drinking and watching television, all to avoid the dark parts of myself that I did not want to face. I knew exactly how much I could drink and still be able to somewhat function at work the next day. But if I wanted to get sober, maybe I'd have to start showering without a drink. It seemed silly and pointless to bring a nonalcoholic drink in the shower, seeing how juice didn't really provide the same buzz.

Something shifted inside of me that morning on Memorial Day. I was ready for change. I was ready to love myself-all parts of myself. Alcohol had been the one thing that helped me fill the void, helped me stop feeling my feelings. Giving it up was facing the unknown. I felt lonely. It felt scary, but I knew it was time to start feeling my *real* feelings, no matter how emotionally painful it was.

In the beginning, I tried to get sober on my own. It only took me three weeks to realize I was going to need professional help, so I found a counselor. As a teen, I'd already experienced Alcoholics Anonymous from a court order from an underage drinking ticket, and there was no way I was going back there. The experience had made me uncomfortable. I remember an older gentleman telling me, "Someday you'll come back here because you want to." At the time, I did not believe him.

Counseling was a comfort for me. It gave me hope and helped me devise a plan. It was nice to have someone listen. It helped me to get real with myself and fully admit where I was in my life and where I wanted to go. But my feelings changed when she told me it was time to go to AA and get a sponsor. In fact, she insisted. I listened.

My experience in AA was an important part of my journey, but it was just the beginning. AA was the place I realized some people understood how I felt. It's the place I worked through a 12-step program with my sponsor. It's the place where I learned to find my connection to my higher power. It's the place I stood up and told my story, when getting my one-year chip. It's the place where I said, "I'm Jessica. I'm an alcoholic," over and over. It's also the place I decided it didn't feel good to say, "I'm an alcoholic" anymore.

I had an amazing sponsor who taught me a lot about staying sober. However, the greatest lesson she taught me she probably didn't even realize. After 18 months in the program, one day she called and told me she had to let me go. She felt I wasn't doing the work or the program the way it was intended to be. I wasn't "showing up" in a sense. She said, "I can't do the work for you." I didn't know what to say or do. I remember sitting in my car and crying. I felt alone and betrayed. I didn't understand. I felt like I was doing my best and it just wasn't enough. But, if I was completely honest, I didn't want to be in the program anymore. I wasn't enjoying the meetings. What once felt like support, became a chore and something I dreaded. Several years later, I was able to look back and know that letting go was the greatest thing she taught me. I know it was hard for her to let me go, but I am glad she did, and I have so much respect for her for doing so.

I never went to a meeting again. I'm not saying that AA meetings are pointless. I'm simply saying to follow your heart and trust yourself. There are many paths to recovery, so follow your path. That can mean using AA, it can mean using part of it, or it can mean another journey entirely. It's okay to outgrow something and expand and heal in other ways-if that's what you feel intuitively led to do. I am grateful for this experience. It taught me that it's okay to leave something that no longer serves me or my highest good if I'm continuously committed to doing what is best for my recovery path. I found that letting go was a natural part of growth and change.

After AA, one thing I knew for sure, was that I was once again on a new part of my journey, still sober, finding my way. Today, I say, "I am sober. I am healing." I'm so glad I finally listened to that voice inside of me that said, "Give up alcohol and your life will change." It has changed. It's still changing. Life isn't perfect, but it gets better and better. I'm equally glad that I listened to the voice that said, "There is more than one path to recover." My recovery path soon evolved into my spiritual path as I turned to other support groups, meditation, journaling, spiritual mentors, and like-minded people. I continued to follow my intuition and listen to my heart. Eventually, I found myself in a position where I could guide and help others, by creating support groups and offering card readings.

You can let go of what no longer serves you. Maybe it's drugs or alcohol. Maybe it's another form of addiction or habit. Whatever it is, you can let go. Trust yourself. You can move forward, and you can heal.

JessSpiritual@gmail.com

jessicaloper.com

FB.com/JessicaSpiritual

FB.com/InspiringRecovery

Free to Be Me

By D. Trifanya Osei

Growing up, it was hard not knowing how life could be so sweet without any abuse. I was so determined to be healed and be a very happy person. I wanted to experience smiling through the day just like everyone else. So, I began my healing journey at the age of 26.

Throughout this process I found it necessary to isolate myself from those who caused me the most pain, but also friends and family who were in my corner. This was necessary to eliminate all the outer noises that suppressed the inner voices I needed to process my experiences from childhood to adult.

If you've ever experienced trauma living throughout most of your adolescent years and trying to operate as a high functioning adult, it can be scary or adventurous depending on your personality. For me, it was both. It was scary because I was so used to being called all sorts of names other than what was on my birth certificate. I had suffered being exposed to physical violence (this is called being a secondary victim) watching my mother being beaten. I had also went being abused as a child physically, emotionally, verbally, spiritually, and sexually. None of these things attributed to me being well in the future. It got to the point that all I thought I was good for was fighting through the day and making sure my two younger sisters were safe, even if I had to put myself in harm's way to keep them from getting hurt. I wasn't accustomed to abuse free living.

As an adult, while going through my healing process, I met so many great new friends. Their support gave me such a great perspective on life, and I began to smile more and frown less because I was surrounded by individuals who had not experienced what I went through. Their experiences were more ideal and "future tensed."

Being "future tensed" is what kept me striving for my goals when it looked as if they were never going to be accomplished. Future tensed is when you are so focused on where you're going that you tend to, sometimes, lose sight of where you have been. For a small length of time, that was necessary for me. At least until I married later in life at the age of 45. I never wanted to marry early because there was so much I wanted to achieve before then like traveling, finish college, and starting my own business. Those were all checked on my list before saying that famous "I do."

A year and a half into the marriage is when things turned sour. I became a victim of Intimate Partner Violence known as Domestic Violence. At first, I was just as upset with myself because I had worked so hard on being healed and enjoying life. How could I NOT see the flags? You know what? You won't always see the red flags. Some people are so strategic with camouflaging and we also tend to forget that just because there are classic signs of abuse known, there are so many others that only come with your personal experiences with the abuser victimizing you.

Fast forwarding, I ran away one night after being beaten and strangled. I was seen by a Forensic Nurse and a very patient Officer who assisted me with everything I needed to feel safe. I gave myself one week to deal with my emotions as soon as I went home after my husband was picked up by the local authorities. After that week, I brushed myself off and got to work. I began using my coping techniques I had picked up from Psychologists and Psychiatrists I had worked with years ago, and also utilized some I developed as a child. As a result, I completed my Master's in Business, reopened my business, hired a Bookkeeper (who has become my biggest cheerleader), published two books, became a serial advocate with a podcast I started in October 2019 discussing Domestic Violence, Child Abuse, Sexual Violence, and Suicide Prevention as it relates to abuse. I am now working on books 3, 4, and 5 while preparing for numerous interviews as a result of my story, podcast, and publications.

Being healed from a life of abuse is tedious, but very possible. There is a lot of strategizing that goes into it. I know firsthand how daunting it is and can help you through this process. Here is a list that can help you think what you can do:

1. Decide if you really want to leave. Once you do this, it is easier to know what it is you need to do for you (and children if you have any).

2. Decide if you want to stay in your area or move. This is very important to know for #3.

3. Create a plan of escape. Creating a plan involves how you can escape safely with or without children. Most people believe you can just walk right out of an abusive situation. Not true. You have to plan your way out. The abuser is not willing to lose you and will do everything in their power to keep you in a victim state.

4. Gather important information (Birth certificate, financial accounts, immunization records, etc) – to ease the stress of possibly losing them, you can take photos of each of these things and send them to a bogus email your abuser has no idea about. Make sure you erase the history of the email after going into it and be sure to sign out of it every time you use it. You don't want the abuser to know about the account.

5. Locate your local YWCA and United Way organizations. They are helpful with resources when you are not financially able to get where you need to go in the event of a crisis.

6. If you have someone you trust who your husband is not friends with (nor ever will be), include that person in your escape plan. If you don't have such a person, call your local YWCA and tell them you need to speak with someone about leaving an abusive situation. They are able to support you whether you want to remain in the area or be housed someplace safe until you are able to move in another area.

7. Journal, journal, and journal some more. In your bogus email, write yourself letters as if you are writing to your best friend saving their life and tell them all the wonderful plans they had told you about they wanted to fulfill. Remind yourself (in these letters) how important you are and that you are very much needed on the healed side of life. Doing this last thing is what put me in the right mindset to follow through with my plans to a healed life.

I am extremely happy because not only am I healed, but I am also in a place of supporting others to their happy place, safely. Can you do the same? YES YOU CAN! Just remember, each case is different. The plans you make are strategically for you and your children's safety.

Website: https://www.linktr.ee/ElegantGranny

Instagram, Twitter, & Periscope: @elegantgranny

Facebook: 1ElegantGranny

LinkedIn: https://www.linkedin.com/in/dtrifanyaosei/

Podcast: bit.ly/proactiveeye

Love & Extra Love

By RayTara Black

She sat on the carpet that smelled fresh in her walk-in closet hoping not to be found. She cuddled and hid herself between the hanging clothes. She didn't want to be found. As she hid between the clothes, she could smell the lavender softener that she uses when she washed. Then suddenly she thought, *how did she get there?*

How did she get to the point in her marriage where she had to hide from her husband? She sat in the closet in so much physical pain. She had no way to attend to her bruises and bleeding. She felt helpless because at that point, she was helpless.

She could hear his feet stooping around on the freshly refurbished hardwood floors. He, her husband, was going back and forth. Then sometimes the sound would fade away and come back. Was she doomed? She did not know what to do. She was beyond frightened and didn't know what the next steps would bring. Her mind drifted off to her daughters. She worried about who would raise them in the event something happened to her. She worried because she knew no one could raise them like her. They needed her, their mother.

While in isolation in the closet, it made her think back. Think back to her past relationships with men. What could possibly be wrong with her to the point that she became their punching bag?

Twenty-five years ago she encountered her first domestic violence experience. She had had a terrific and fun night out with her friends. They danced and laughed the night away. She was heading home and just a block away from her turn when she discovered a familiar black car sitting in the middle of a double lane street. Blocking both east and west lanes. She couldn't get pass. Upon further inspection, it was him, her boyfriend. The look in his eyes were like fire and she could feel the heat in her car.

She begged and pleaded through the window to let her pass and they would meet in front of her house. He accepted and let her pass as he made a U-turn behind her to follow. He drove so close to the back of her that she could no longer see his headlights. The drive seemed like forever and she was scared and trembling. *What would happen next?* She thought once they met in front of the home.

They made it to the front of her house. She was still terrified of what would happen next. This was a face she never saw before. He appeared to be the size of a bear looking down at her. His arms curled in a front position to grab her and he did. With great force, she never knew his gentle touch as she was lifted and was thrown to the ground. She could feel the dirt move under her hands as she helplessly made it to the ground. Her entire body was in the dirt. She laid there, hoping it was and her only unknown punishment. At that moment, her hoping failed her. She rose to her feet just to be pushed into her car and getting hit. She tried to fight also, but to her the hits were like a baby's touch to his forceful hits. After a few blocks of swerving down the street at high speed and fighting, he took her glasses and pushed her out the car. She rolls and rolls against the concrete. Scratching her knees and body as she rolled, she moved to the curve and sat there crying. *How could this be?* It wasn't even her car. It was her mother's She was just puzzled. Not being able to see, she cried and walked home squinting, barely seeing where she was going. She stumbled and fell repeatedly over objects in the street and on the sidewalks until she made it home.

Today she, RayTara Black, walks with her head held high, confident in every step and purposeful with every word. Why? I came to the conclusion that I would have to lose a lot to gain more and that's what I did. I constantly repeated two Scriptures, "I can do all things through Christ who strengthens me" Philippians 4:13 and "For I know the plans I have for you" declares the Lord. "Plans to prosper you and not to harm you, plans to give you hope and a future" Jeremiah 29:11. I repeated this until it became my mantras, my affirmations, my all. Then the day came when I had the strength and just left it all. My husband, my car, my house, and everything in it. There I was, bare without anything but the clothes I had on and my daughters' school uniforms. That was it for me and I was willing to lose it all for the sake of me and my daughters. We deserved more. I felt like a bag of bricks were lifted off my back. The sun felt hotter and the day seemed brighter as I thought about my next steps. But, before I left the house and all in it, I left a poem on our bed which was now his. It read.

<u>Courage</u>

My courage speaks out

From behind my smile.

You can hit, stomp, and choke me,

But I won't hold my head down,

Because just as I know;

The night brings the moon

I know that your life and misery

Will cause me no more gloom.

For I have a future

As bright as the sun.

Your cloudy days of forever rains

Are just no longer fun.

It's utterly amazing

When one can wake up and walk away

From everything she's once had

To look forward to a better day.

There are still monkeys on the back.

They are just different ones now.

As I must figure out a new way of life;

What to do and how.

The physical pain is gone away

And can't be seen anymore.

But the mental anguish and memories

Makes me question what I would come back for.

I am a priceless treasure,

And deserve to be treated as one

So, I look forward to rich filled days,

Because I know we are over and dome.

Once gone, there was a newfound freedom that I hadn't had in years. I started exercising, practicing yoga, writing poems, and communicating with my family and friends again. My faith never wavered as I knew God was working within me. I could only go up from being at the bottom with nothing, not even a job. I continued to pray and say my mantras, my affirmations, my all.

Within a few months, I found an apartment without having a job. I stood firm and told the landlord I had a custom cake bakery business and that was my only source of income. However, at the time, I didn't have one customer but I believed in myself and knew that I didn't come this far for nothing. That's where the birth of Sweet Dreams Events, Décor and More was made. I decided to be a one-stop-event-shop and it's still going strong.

Now I find myself talking to other domestic violence individuals about my triumphs and how I preserved. Most importantly to show them there is a rainbow at the end of the storm even after everything seems gone. Hopefully my story of successfully making it to have my own business through the battle of recovery would encourage others to sometimes if possible to walk away.

312-813-0110
sweetdreamseventschicago.com
owner@sweetdreamseventschicago.com

When Life Tries to Knock You Out

By Twahki Rhodes

When life tries to knock you out! Think of someone that you know that is thirteen or remember when you yourself was thirteen. The number thirteen represents combined energy of numbers one and three. It is a number with very strong symbolism and has great power. One has a vibration of new ideas, new beginnings, process, and individually. Three symbolizes passion, motivation, optimism, self-expression, and inspiration. It is the age of transformation, I remember I was changing from adolescent to teen. My body was weird, my emotions were on a roller-coaster, I was noticing boys more too. Because of curiosity, sneaking and snooping, I started trying to find out what this sex thing was. As a child, things happened that might have steered me on this course, needless to say, I went to my mom and told her as if I was big and bad, "So mom I got something to tell you." "What?" she replied "I'm ready to have sex." A pause with a look like she swallowed a can followed. Then she said, "I think you should wait on that. Not now, can you wait?" I caught her by surprise, my mouth said yes, but my mind was still curious. I wasn't just out looking to have sex now; NO.

I rejected a lot of little horny teens looking to score their first. Not me, I wanted that 80's teen love story. One boy caught my eye, he wasn't into anything but dancing, which was cool cause I loved to dance, I pounced soon as I had a chance. I threw everything out of the 12th floor window, I did it scared and all. Not thinking of course of the aftermath, and all that came with doing it.

My mom noticed the sanitary pads were the same count, she asked me about it, I was dumbfounded like: *Huh? What are you talking about?* She said, "Have you come on your period? I said, "No." She said, "When was the last time?" I said, "I don't know." I had no clue about keeping up with it, and the 28-day thing, just lost. The next thing I knew, I didn't have to go to school, I got a doctor's appointment. We get there and my mom is telling me about my appointment, this wasn't going to be my regular checkup. I was scared only cause I had to undress and let all see me on this cold table, I felt so naked and alone. A good-looking man came in to examine me. This was not something I could have ever thought happened to women, then with me still naked on this table, a nurse came in to say, "Her test was positive. She is pregnant!" All the smiling and politeness my mom had went out the door, hello Ms. Preordination, young single black mom. It hit the fan! She went off quietly because she didn't want people in our business, but I heard her loud and clear, the looks and words pierced. From that moment on from that cold table I felt as if I was the worst thing ever. I felt worthless, less than and very ugly. I was never an outgoing person to begin with, but this dimmed any light that I had mounted on top of the kicks before, this crowned the insecurities like a cherry on top.

The only great thing about this whole ordeal is what was growing in my womb. I was looked at by people as my stomach grew. The looks were of discuss, shame, hate, and disbelief; among that, whispers and pointing followed. This was a time when the media came up with the slogan: "Babies having babies." It was plastered everywhere. In 1986, there was a TV broadcast every few minutes that seemed like, a PBS movie was made, even a song of such shame. Even though women have been getting married and pregnant since the beginning of time, it was very looked down upon in the 21st century, even in the alternative school where I went for girls; we got teased by the high school girls. I had to catch the bus downtown to school every day. One day as I was riding a very packed bus as it usually was, I had to stand up, I was about seven or eight months at the time. As people were getting on, I got pushed closer to the man sitting in front of me. He pushed back hard in my stomach, I looked around to see who saw what he had done, but there were only looks of: *You deserve what you get.* That hurt my spirit and crushed my soul. Yes, I was pregnant and a child, but did I deserve such hatred?

I turned 14, gave birth, and graduated with my son just five months in the front row looking on. Years later, I am still very insecure and beat down, but happy and blessed with two grown children and grandchildren, through all the kicks, insecurities, being constantly put down, and looked down upon. The poem, *Still I Rise* by Maya Angelou comes to mind, but it was all Elshaddi's work. Thanks, and glory be to my Father who art in Heaven, because my rejection was His divine protection. Where I was weak and felt defeated, God picked me up and was my peace and strength. You see before I surrendered to really seek after God, I kept allowing my downfall, I kept running back to hurt, not knowing He had always been there covering me protecting me, picking me up, and dusting me off. When the world kept bullying, He was my refuge, my strong tower. I can truly look back and see how He did not allow me to die. I had to fight for me, for my family, for my future with the strength He gave me. I had to fight daily for sanity. His Word states: ...that he had not given me a spirit of fear but of power, love, and a sound mind.

Our minds are amazing brilliant organs that God created so intricate, so matchless we were created in His image. Just as He willed it to be for us to make decisions, our minds will talk back to us, it can lie and deceive you. Hurts, actions, things said replay over and over, but you must fight. I had to continually tell myself the opposite of what the world said about me and what I said about myself in ignorance. I could no longer meditate on the negative cause. It will rule your life. What you continue to replay in your mind will play you! When I realized that from adolescence to now; I had years of hurt, of damage, of insecurities, and failures. I had to dig my mind out of, I had to constantly talk to myself, uplift myself, prophesy over myself, and speak positivity into my life. I had to celebrate the beautifully, uniquely, wonderfully, fearfully, creatively made Child of the most High that is, TWAHKI!

twahkirhodes@gmail.com

www.facebook.com/twahki

You Can Begin Again

By Michelle Garrett

"This moment doesn't define you. You're not the first person who has been at this point, and you won't be the last. What matters most is what you do next. You've been given the opportunity to begin again. Never take that for granted."

Have you experienced a moment that you just knew was life-changing? When you just knew that your journey would forever be impacted for better or worse? Oftentimes when we're faced with these events, we are not in a mindset to change course or just pause and think about how our next actions will impact us and our loved ones. Once the adrenaline stops and the moment has passed, it's then that we take the time to take stock of what's happened. We can reflect on the things we could have or should have done, but it's over. We're left to deal with the reality of our actions.

I know this feeling oh-too-well. For years, I ignored the unsettling feeling that something was "off" in my life. My focus and attention were on my family, business, community, friends-everything but me. I felt like a fraud so many times, speaking to women on the importance of loving themselves, putting their needs first, and creating a routine that included self-care. Those were all things that in the past I had made a priority. As I slipped deeper into depression, they fell lower and lower on my list of priorities.

Depression truly gives a false sense of reality to your circumstances. The issue is you can't see the true view until you're out of your depressive state. No matter what others say or do, your mind believes what it believes. Over time, I drew what seemed like rational conclusions based on my mindset.

I found a way to trace back every negative thing in my life, my family's life, and my business to me and my ineptitude. After a while, the logical conclusion was to remove myself from the equation.

When you hit absolute rock bottom, there's hope and possibility in the escape. Often you feel as though you have exhausted all of the options and choices you have. Yes, I reached out to multiple loved ones. I had gotten so used to not prioritizing and valuing my feelings and emotions, that I could not adequately express the agony I was experiencing. I was the strong one. That person that everyone depended on. How could I be facing something I did not know how to manage?

I had thought through the ramifications of my actions. A detailed plan was in place to ensure my family's life continued seamlessly. Of course, now that I am in a place of healing, I realize how flawed my thinking was. There are moments when the thought of the pain I caused them, hurts more than the years of depression I endured. But ...we all began again.

I wish I could say it was a Hallmark movie ending, it wasn't. Almost a year later, we're still healing and making amends. There are times when the simplest gesture triggers emotions and feelings that take us reeling back to that time apart.

Open communication makes a difference. The conversations that I have with my eight-year-old are definitely not the conversations my mother and I had. However, I need to give her a safe space. A place to let me know when she's fearful, confused, or sad. The same goes for everyone in my household. Growing up, my Daddy always said the most important people in my life are the people who lived within our four walls. That point was driven home for me last year.

In order to begin again, I had to start with my foundation. My faith, my healing, my overall well-being became my main priority. I can remember my husband and parents stressing that they only wanted me to think about myself. They would take care of everything else. It was not easy to surrender completely, but I did. I am thankful for the support system I have that made that possible. I recognize that not everyone has that in their lives.

I learned the importance of letting those around me know when I'm not feeling 100% and need time to regroup or recharge. It took some time for me to let go of the "superwoman" facade I had gotten used to putting on. Vulnerability isn't easy for me, but it's tied to the level of trust and safety I feel in that moment. When everything is broken down, trust and faith are all you have to depend on.

My circle has shifted and changed tremendously. People I thought would always be there for me ... weren't. And I was surprised by some that did show up. That helped me re-evaluate the time and energy I was putting into, honestly, everything. It's not a quid pro quo relationship, by any means. I focus more on who and what brings me joy and satisfaction. There are times when I am just drawn to certain people-whether it's to listen, share bits of my story or just be there. There's power in being present. Not feeling as though action needs to be taken, but just being in the moment.

The words my discharge nurse shared with me have stayed with me over the months. Moments don't define us. How we grow and change afterwards do. Every day I have to make a decision to get up and choose to be present. Some days are easier than others. But each day I remember that I can begin again.

www.divaswithapurpose.com

MichelleDGarrett1@gmail.com

You Can Transform

By Tonia Reaves

I Am Tonia Survives. My story, although very common, is also one that a lot of people suffer in silence about. My purpose is not to give you a long novel about what happened to me. However, my goal in this project is to let you know that you can transform into who you were proposed to be. The ugly things that happened to you were meant to do two things. God used it to make you strong. He is the essential reason that you are still here. The enemy tried to use your situation to destroy you.

I know people question why God would allow you to be hurt. I had those same questions. It was the "Why me?" questions, blaming everyone including myself. *If I wasn't so weak then this. If I had told my parents, then that. If I had slept in my parent's room, then.* I was sexually abused from the time I was four until around 10 years old. I began to hate who I saw in the mirror. All of my flaws were highlighted. If someone complimented me, I felt as though they were not being honest.

I think of how a butterfly transforms from this ugly, slimy creature, into this beautiful exquisite creature with wings. I compare that to our lives. We go through dark situations that make us feel we are going through the four stages of the butterfly's life cycle. The beginning is the eggs, then larvae. This is the slimy, not so attractive phase. We eventually become the Pulpa. The Pulpa is like a cocoon. This is when you realize where all of the hurt and guilt came from and what it was for. God is revealing things to you about yourself, the things that you experienced, and how to heal from them. Some people go through a phase when they begin purging off all that was meant to fall away. Underneath it all, is your beautiful wings that will help you to fly. That's when you realize God has taken off the limits. It's when He helps you to see what He sees.

He created us to be loving, vibrant, and beautiful beings. We go through situations as we struggle with temptations and trying to do the right things in life. We struggle with hearing from God and battling our flesh. Those experiences were designed to press us into our designed purpose. Eventually, we find ourselves as close to being in alignment with His Word, purposes, and plans for our lives as we'll ever be. We will continue to grow as we pour into others. Our job is to learn, grow, reach, and teach. That is the intended cycle of our lives. It's not always the best feeling. It is sometimes the most painful. As we allow God to lead us, the pain is not so noticeable.

toniasurvives@gmail.com

~~Un~~Loveable

By Lisa Madden

From the very beginning, there were odds stacked against me. I was born to an unwed teenage mother, who had to endure physical and emotional abuse from the father of her child. Not only was I born into rejection and despair, but in poverty living on the fifteenth floor of a south side project in Chicago. I can remember moments of happiness and feelings of love when I was in the presence of my grandmother, Annie. She saw the need early on to shield me from certain pain.

Walking into the rust-colored office with the cherry oak wood desk with this figure behind it, seemed like a giant. I was alone, uncertain, and afraid of what was about to happen.

I had gotten into trouble with my father at home, which caused me to have to receive one of his many brutal whippings. Once in school, my teacher and one of my close friends noticed blood on my face. My teacher asked me where the blood came from and my friend yelled out in front of the entire class "Did your dad do that to you?" I became mortified and wanted to shrink down into a hole right there. I gave her the look of shut up, please. My teacher immediately began questioning me about my father and what had happened. All my teachers knew what was happening at home, but never really interfered, just listened when I needed to talk. Not this time. There was a cut on my face, and he claimed he couldn't ignore it. I pleaded with him to let me go to my class, but he insisted on taking me to the guidance office. Not only were the authorities called, but my mother too. I didn't know how to handle what was happening, I just pretended everything was okay. Later in the school day, I got another call to come to the office where I entered a room where my mother sat with tear stains dried on her face. I didn't want to look at her, not because her face scared me, but because looking at her face would make me want to protect her. She asked to take me home with her, and we left the school. The ride home was silent and filled with tears. Once we got home, she wanted to know why, as if she was clueless to what had occurred that morning. We argued about her willful ignorance and need to protect her marriage, but this was a battle I felt I had to win, and determined to do so.

She took me to the church for reinforcements to get me to change my mind about the report I made.

I sat down in front of his desk, and he stares at me for awhile, straight through my soul. "So, what's going on?" he asked? I responded, "Nothing." He asked, "Are you sure? That's not what I'm hearing." "I'm tired of being beat for nothing." He stared and looked at me for what seemed to be forever, then he uttered the very words that would change the course of my life. "You know you have always been a difficult child. Very unlovable." My eyes went blank and filled with tears, my heart sank into my stomach. I was no longer in the room. I could see myself in my chair, see him hand me a tissue, but I didn't hear any sound coming out of his mouth. I floated around the room and could hear him say, "Your mother has a hard time loving you." He threw more daggers at me, and I couldn't understand why my mom didn't love me. By the meeting's end, I'd agreed to retract my statement to the police and child services for him, telling my father to stop beating me as much.

Life didn't get any better for me after that, actually harder. I got pushed aside, ostracized, mistreated, rejected, shamed, and violated way into my adulthood. My childhood trauma shaped the way I saw people, dealt with people, and tried to learn from people. I couldn't trust or love properly, but I constantly sought after them both, vigorously. I sat in church week after week, watching my father preach of a love from God so deep that no man could understand. How that the souls of a man was important to God, yet I felt like I didn't matter to anyone, not even God. These constant feelings of disconnection caused me to seek love whenever I could find it outside my home and the house of God, because all my pain was there. Ultimately, I became a teenage unwed mother, and this led to even more shaming and black balling.

I learned to defend myself, sometimes unhealthily, but it was the only way I could feel safe, protected. I become a champion for anyone I felt was an underdog.

After a failed suicide attempt, I realized I had to be special to God, that maybe I had a purpose and just maybe He loved me, that I wasn't too dirty for Him.

My journey started there in the psych ward, where I heard God's voice tell me I was special to Him. But it wasn't until I was pregnant with my last child, I overcame those feelings of being unlovable.

It was during that pregnancy I searched my soul and ran after God with everything I had in me that wasn't broken to give Him. I knew God's grace was sufficient. By no means did I try to glorify my sin, but I embraced the fact that terrible things had happened to me as a child that shaped my mindset and thought process. I learned that certain traumas and word curses caused me to believe I wasn't good enough for the love of God, that I was dirty and unworthy.

I learned that in all my sins and adversity, God was with me every step of the way. He kept me sane and constantly showed me tremendous love in small and large gestures. I knew then that I meant everything to Him no matter my faults or what I'd done. I had His heart whenever I was ready to open myself up to my healing process.

He talked to me and listened to me when others didn't think I was good enough to even fight for. God fought for me.

He began showing me the pain that shaped my past behavior was not the real me. It was the puppet'd me. The real me emerged and came to life. Now she's showing herself strong. No longer listening to those voices that said I would not make it.

But I survived it all. I lived to tell the story of trauma, triumph, and now my healing.

Now I am the voice that God has chosen to be the light and salt to others who need their stories of being a preacher's kid told.

I did...

I call this phase the "I did" phase because it comes after you have completed something. It's the phase after everything on the checklist, for the moment, is done. It's the time when the goal is achieved, or what you've thirst for has been obtained. In this phase, you should be proud, for it is here where you've won your first round with failure. I personally like the "I did" phase. It's when one realizes they have some triumphs under their belt. For example, I bask in the ambiance of the "I did" phase when I received my Bachelor's degree. It was something I set out to do and it came to pass. My I cans turned into I did. It is here when you get a little taste of success. It's when you feel one step closer to self-actualization and overall fulfilment; however, I warn you of its side effects. A dosage of the "I did" phase can be vigorous to winning the second round with failure.

Why? I'm glad you asked.

When in the "I did" phase one gets a little taste of accomplishment; therefore, they may become complacent with where they are in life. The "I did" phase is where you are able to see your progress. You are able to see how far you've come. It is in this phase where you may even compare some of the things you've achieved to your peers or others your age, and/ or in your position. In the "I did" phase you can become comfortable, but as I am writing this, I warn you to not become friends with comfortability. With comfortability comes a lackadaisical spirit. In comfortability, one can become blind to the greater things, for even the best can become better. Take this for intense. As I stated before, I received my Bachelor's degree. The "I can," turned into I did, but that was years ago. I graduated in 2018. I looked around at my former peers and realized I had a better grip on life than some; however, I have still become a prisoner to comfortability. I thought I would go right on to get my Master's, and even obtain a doctorate degree. It was only when I realized that I was not overcoming failure, but sustaining in it. I knew more had to be done, and even though I haven't gone back to school yet, I have become aware of this costume that fear of failing disguised itself in.

As we are continuously overcoming failure, and the fear of failing, it is important to remember that failure is something that is always sneaking up on us. I once heard: "When you go to a higher level, you must fight a different devil." This means, you have to keep fighting and pressing to a higher level. I want you to know that the "I did" phase is truly a frenemy. It's both good and bad. Yes, you made it happen, but you made it happen for the time of yesterday. Once you get this in your head, you will find yourself thinking higher, and becoming higher simultaneously. So, I encourage you to always make it happen for today, tomorrow, and ever more. See yourself as higher. See yourself as being able to do anything. Never let anyone tell you that you can't fly. And if they do, send them a picture of a plane ticket. You can do more, so celebrate in the I did phase, but don't hesitate to leave it. You can, for yesterday. You did, for today. And tomorrow you will.

lisamadden1107@gmail.com

Move Beyond Shameful Past and Into a More Meaningful Future

By Julie Jordan Scott

More than twenty years ago, I sat in a therapist's office and she asked me to make a list of "Family Rules," which I went home and wrote. I returned with my list with lots of blue ink across a yellow legal pad. My cursive lettering detailed unspoken codes of conduct such as "Don't cry in public" and "Do not do things that might embarrass the family."

There is space in the world for such guidelines.

I don't agree with any prohibition on crying-perhaps because I am one who cries at movie previews, coffee commercials, and baptisms of people I don't even know. It isn't the rules themselves that causes the problems all these years later, it is in the denial of what happened because of these unspoken codes.

What I believe in is taking back our personal power through creative process and growth. It isn't about blaming others or fault-finding or pointing fingers-it is about acknowledging our own strength and truth.

Today, I look back at things that happened when I journal or speak to groups or share blog posts and I write or say, "I am not rewriting history, I am recognizing we are all human and everyone was doing the best they could at the time."

The reality doesn't subtract or nullify the pain that was experienced or the grief that occasionally rears its head, especially during trying times like the COVID-19 pandemic.

Denial, for example, is something we see across social media. It shows up in zoom calls I am on, in conversations with friends and family. Somehow we think if we don't watch the news, COVID-19 will go away. We think if we share "Positivity Only!" on Instagram the situations that plague us will magically disappear. Sometimes we hope and pray reality will happen only to other people.

Denial doesn't bring about true personal power and truth, though. It causes more pain and more struggle and oftentimes more shame.

Sometimes we are ashamed to say we are afraid. You may even be ashamed of feeling ashamed! You may find writing your thoughts in a journal or on pieces of paper you burn or throw away may help begin your healing. You may feel better by reading books by Brene Brown or watching her popular Ted Talks about Shame or reading your Bible.

Brene Brown's work is about working through shame. Not denying it, not burying it, not climbing on top of a pile of lies you made up to look at the view below. Being truthful about shame and grief helps to dismantle shame and see it for what it is.

Making that list of rules all those years ago allowed me to begin to disassemble the rules that didn't fit me and my moral code and choose what was worth saving.

Some of those old family rules were fool's gold or just not right for me.

I aim to consistently be open with my children, ready to talk about issues others turned from or stifled. Recently my son was angry with me and when I said to him, "I am glad you talk to me about these things. My Mom never let me talk to her like this."

Sometimes certain topics: death, grief, job loss, financial trauma, and sexuality are just the beginnings of topics we may have varying levels of discomfort discussing around the dinner table. This last Christmas season, my family gathered around the table and played a conversation game about goals and visions for the year to come. One of our family members would not address any of the questions.

My guess is there was quite a bit of shame attached. The rest of us gave permission for the questions to not be answered.

My hope is the unspoken answers to the questions will continue to percolate.

For some of us, journaling or free writing or writing poetry or songs is the best first way to "talk about" whatever is bringing up feelings of shame.

We will all feel better-and the world will continue healing–when we begin to talk about the things that make us uncomfortable. Once you begin to let your words stop rattling around your brain and start working through your heart onto the page, your vision will become clearer and your pain will lessen.

You will stop feeling shame over the small stuff and begin to build bridges with the people who aren't quite ready to speak up yet.

Here's what I know: Our time is now to move beyond whatever is holding us back. Chances are if you are living, there are some shame experiences to review and set aside, and in some cases, finally bring out into the open so they may be filled with light. The best part is you may begin to write new rules for your family or your community or your group or your church that are not based in shame but are based in healing and love.

juliejordanscott@gmail.com

website creativelifemidwife.com

Facebook.com/JJsWritingCamp

Instagram.com/juliejordanscott

Overcoming The Boogeyman

By Michelle R. Jackson

My name, Michelle Renee, means "who is like God, restored." But from birth to thirty years old, my life resembled that of one who was like the boogeyman, terror-filled, monstrous and destructive. However, I didn't begin in fear-entrenched turmoil.

As a young child I was hopeful, and because of responsibilities assigned to me by my young single mother, I was wise beyond my years. I was not raised in church and had no real understanding of who God was. I was an only child (or so I thought) and a latchkey kid and I experienced lingering loneliness and craved attention, acceptance, and adoration. In fact, to force attention from my mother, I began stealing and lying. Of course, that was counter-productive, but at the very least, I felt seen. Unless I was doing something wrong, I felt invisible. Little did I know, I could feel invisible even when I'm the main attraction. To this day, some attention, I wish I never received.

At nine years old, I was molested by my favorite uncle, and it completely devastated my life. At that moment, my nine-year-old self was destroyed. I felt betrayed because I loved that uncle so much and, if that wasn't traumatic enough, disclosing the sexual assault caused me to be physically assaulted by my aunt. Those events would set the internal atmosphere for the birth of clinical depression and thoughts of suicide. Daily I remember feeling trapped in a cold, dark prison in my own mind. From the age of nine to twelve years old, I considered ending my life almost daily. Then when I was twelve, I attempted suicide. I can't recall if I wanted to die or just wanted someone to be my advocate. What I know for sure is that my value was tied to who would fight for me, and no one fought for me. So, I felt disposable. I thought my life didn't matter. But for some reason, I was drawn to visit a neighborhood church on Sundays without adult supervision. I was desperately seeking hope.

When I was sixteen years old, in addition to being depressed, I began having Grand Mal Seizures. And almost simultaneously, my father, who was incarcerated since I was six years old for raping a young girl, returned into my life. Despite knowing why my father was imprisoned, I thought he would value and love me. I hoped, through some miracle, he would rescue me from a life of insignificance and indifference to a life of love and acceptance. To my chagrin, I would be further victimized because he raped and physically assaulted me. That trauma heightened the depression and suicide ideation. Every second, I wanted to die and attempted suicide again at sixteen and seventeen years old. I was eventually diagnosed with clinical depression and forced to dwell in a mental health facility for eight days. I never knew the daunting face of terror until I was institutionalized in that hospital. The Psychosomatic and Psychiatric Institute is where I would meet the boogeyman, I was seventeen years old.

Soon after my release from the hospital and being raped once more by my father, he was arrested for bank robbery. That was thirty-one years ago, and he is still serving a federal prison sentence today. Clinical depression, mental pain, and thoughts of suicide continued throughout my teens and twenties. Then when I was thirty years old, after wearing masks of wholeness, happiness, hopefulness, and contentment, I attempted suicide for the final time. That pivotal moment began the shift that changed my life. Not only did I physically flatline for a few minutes, but I had an extreme encounter while separated from my body. When my spirit returned to my body, after time and various critical people pouring into me, I realized that a great deal of my life's torment was created by me.

Finally, I started to understand that, yes, the pain and effects of adverse childhood experiences and childhood trauma were real, but long after I was free from others hurting me, I became my own boogeyman. So, what do you do when the boogeyman you fear is you? I didn't realize that the boogeyman cannot dwell in the light. So, the longer I covered the scars of trauma by pretending to be someone I wasn't, the more trauma I invited into my life. I never felt good enough for anything or anyone, so I damaged good relationships and formed reasons to isolate myself. I began to victimize myself by slowly destroying my life. I had several abortions, several failed relationships, and, instead of getting help, I simply masked the torment. I was emotionally bruised, physically fake, and spiritually at war.

The boogeyman's role is to torture the person in the dark. The worst part of being bound for me was the delusion it held. After the trauma, I learned to disassociate and bury things so deep within that, at times, I didn't know I was bound. In the last suicide experience, after I flatlined, a voice (the voice of God) asked why I was there. That question helped prepare me to receive the truth that I was self-sabotaging and acting as my own boogeyman. As a victim, I was restricted and limited to exist in a life beneath what God desired and designed for me. That is, until God began to show me that I could be free. I couldn't believe it because I thought I was sentenced to a life of mental bondage, but with prayer and a conversation with a certain pastor, I started facing the truth. The truth was, I needed to be FLPT. I needed to Forgive then the Love I desired could come, then I could walk into my Purpose while I Transformed my thoughts. Talking to that pastor, I was forced to remove the masks and allow the light of truth to emanate from within.

Slowly but surely, the internal boogeyman was destroyed; like sunshine to a vampire, the boogeyman began to disintegrate before my spiritual eyes. Forgiveness served as a night light; Love rushed in like a flashlight; Purpose overflowed like a studio light and Transformative Thoughts illuminated my soul like a floodlight. Being FLPT disarmed the internal boogeyman which created openness for me to receive the HARD truth, which was Healing, Abundance, Restoration and Deliverance. I FLPT HARD and changed my life.

Everything I went through was difficult, unfair, traumatic, painful and, at times, insurmountable. But I am no longer a victim. I finally realized and received my power, in that, as the Bible says, I can do all things through Christ Jesus who strengthens me.

The boogeyman tried to destroy me, and I tried to destroy me; but God called me to purpose. And, guess what? HE loves and has called you to purpose too! I am certain that NO thing can separate us from the love of God! God is faithful and just to give us an abundant life when we delight ourselves in Him and show up as our authentic self, then He will give us the desires of our heart. His grace is greater than our sins. If I can overcome the boogeyman, you can overcome anything!

coachmichellejackson@gmail.com

You Can Overcome Grief in Everyday Life

By Renee Hupman

Grief is something so common and leaves no one person immune to it. What I have found is that we do not consider grief in everyday life. It sounds like a simple concept yet, it is so overlooked and therefore underestimated. We know that grief is loss but what loss in everyday life would cause us to have a grief response? Perhaps you have been going through a situation in which you have moved away from what you know, are overcoming an addiction, ended a relationship, have a psychological disorder or found yourself to have a chronic illness. There are so many things that we learn to overcome that I can not possibly list them all. Each situation brings forth a loss and adjustment to our everyday life. Whatever you find yourself in need of overcoming, understand that you can and you will. Yes it will take some adjustment and some work but what will take place as you understand that it is ok to allow yourself to feel the emotions that you have you can start your journey to healing.

The Kubler-Ross model identifies the following as the stages of grief to be a normal response cycle. It is important to know that these stages are not always in order and we may repeat one stage at any time.

Denial

Anger

Bargaining

Depression

Acceptance

I want to take a little time to explain these as I identify these stages in everyday life so that we understand what healing will look like.

Denial

It is very easy to ignore changes in ones life that need to happen in order for you to live in freedom from what holds you down. We are never able to conquer what we will not confront and therefore keep ourselves in a constant motion of doing the same thing over and over. The following are two examples of denial.

Perhaps you have been in an abusive relationship and left only to find yourself in another abusive relationship. If you ask anyone, most likely they will tell you that there were red flags that they ignored in the beginning of any abusive relationship. Denial ultimately will lead to self doubt. More often than not I have found that the testimonies of many of my online ministry viewers start with just that. If we can not love ourselves enough to know what we do and do not deserve we will find ourselves repeating the same cycle.

Maybe you have been dealing with an addiction. Have you told yourself that you can handle this? Would an addiction keep you from dealing with the root issue ? Finding your courage to face addiction can be very tricky as we often see this as drugs or alcohol. Could the addiction be food. Could it be taking over the counter medications to numb the negative thoughts of not feeling good enough so that recovery can not take place?

Anger

No one person likes to be angry. Anger as it applies to grief in everyday life is sometimes a flood of emotions that you may not feel you can verbally say. Anger is grief of what was and what now exist. Anger can be ones inability to move forward if not directed in the correct way. We all have a choice at this stage to continue in the healing. This is where we are certain that life as we know it will change. If we choose to heal in this stage then we must look deeply at what we want the outcome to be. I find it especially helpful to write down your end goal and keep your focus on that. If something or someone in your life does not serve this then they are blocking your healing and blessing . Anger can drive you to receive help, push yourself to be a better person, understand your value and love you. Anger can help you to confront that thing that you were previously in denial about.

Bargaining

At this point we are really in resistance to embrace what we left. If I do this then I can do that. If I have one drink I will not have a problem. If I call my abusive ex husband I will not go back to him because I am stronger now. It sounds so silly to read I am sure but it is all commonly said as a normal statement in this stage. In the Bible God warns us not to turn back from the plow (Luke9:62) . Now I know that some of us have never seen a plow so I will explain this in my own words. When you begin to bargain you are really not wanting to let go of what you knew before. Sometimes we are going through this stage thinking about our youth and the goals we had then. It is important to know that as we evolve our goals shift but if you have not fulfilled your destiny then your bargaining may be reasoning for running from an original goal. If I hold on to a shopping cart and I look back to see what I may have missed then I turn my head and as I do my shoulders begin to shift backward and when I look down so have my feet gone in a backward motion. Suddenly I am upset over the things of the past and what was: even if it was not good for me instead of focusing on what is

Depression

Depression is that nasty little liar that says we will never be good enough. Depression can be amplified by the belief in our own insecurities and doubts. It is that feeling that can push us or pull us. This is where we make a conscious choice that something must change in order to evolve as God has created us to.

When we start to believe the negative things associated with our situation then we begin to lose our battle. If I had said in my twenties that I would never walk again after almost losing my leg and two years of learning to walk I would not be walking today. If I had listened to the statistics and how experimental the multiple surgeries were with little room for a good outcome then I would not have the result I wanted.

Depression can also help us to heal if we let it. You see, at any point in your life you have the ability to rewrite your story. Depression confronted is when our view of the future is a little clouded and we begin to self-evaluate. This is where we sort through our thoughts to find what is true and what will serve us. This is where we begin to realize that God created us and if he created us then we are just as important to him as he is to us. This is where you begin to shake off self doubt and love yourself.

Acceptance

Acceptance is understanding that our life has seasons and we may be walking in to the next one differently than we did at denial yet we have begun a new journey and we accept the new things that come with it. Learning to accept is one of the best things you can do to overcome anything. You decided to show up for today and you decided you were important enough to do so.

For me acceptance was learning to believe that living with chronic pain, almost losing my leg, health issues, PTSD from police injustice, having Celiac Disease and waiting for the right person to come along and getting married against the age society would perceive as normal and starting a road that lead to an online ministry and life as an entrepreneur was going to be my new normal. It never made me immune to pain,but it made me uniquely the evangelist who cares deeply for God's people . I believe that everything I have every gone through has benefited someone else. Acceptance was where I learned to love me and that I was a reflection of God's love. When you begin to accept the full spectrum and love you, that is where you understand that there is so much good inside of you and so much to offer the world. That is what happened for me at acceptance and I hope reading this will lead you to healing and inspiring others as I hope I have done for you.

When you own your truth it then belongs to no one person but you and you alone. We must learn to be ok with us and love ourselves.

Reneesglamstudio@yahoo.com
Glamgravity.com
Fruitfulbranchesministry@yahoo.com
Follow me on all social media at GlamQueenForGod
Fruitful Branches Ministry on Facebook

Been There.... Done THAT!!

By Mikkita Moore

I am Mikkita L Moore. I am a Woman of God FIRST. Mother, Daughter, Friend. I am also an Author, International Transparency Motivator, Tour and Time Management Coach, Event Host, and Facilitator.

I now live, walk, and breathe Transparency...I remember being so very afraid to open up enough to tell my story, because of what other people's thoughts would be about me. I remember how I was always mean, defensive, and ignorant to my own feelings. It was so bad that one day I looked up and I had no clue who the person was standing in the mirror...I saw Her, but not ME. That's the moment I had to make a choice...ME... Or the stranger in the mirror!!!!!

I remember going through what I call the greatest depression. My mother had been diagnosed with breast cancer, my older children and I were at odds with each other, my middle son was running away, robbing people, and in and out of lockup, my baby boy was miserable, and my baby girl was too little to know what was really happening.

When my mother was diagnosed with breast cancer, all I could think about was how I would survive if she were gone. To paint the picture for you, I grew up with a platinum spoon in my mouth, I never had to pay bills or pay for anything I needed. I actually didn't really even know how to pay bills until I moved out of Illinois at the age of 37 years old. So, when I heard my mother had cancer, all I could do was selfishly think to myself: *How will I pay the bills in this house if I lose her?* The second thought was:

But this is my best friend; I can't lose all that I have. At the same time that my mother had her surgery and chemo, I was recovering in a cast from an ankle fracture which resulted in me receiving a plate, five screws, and a pin in my right ankle. I was, to say the least, immobile. It was in all of those events that my older children became what felt like completely defiant. My oldest daughter was starting to not come home at night; spending nights at friends' homes, and I'm sure once or twice with the then boyfriend. She and I was not getting along at all, to say the least. My oldest son and I didn't see eye to eye at all, resulting in me putting my hands on him and having the police called to my home. He subsequently left, not only home, but the city of Chicago as well. We had no contact with each other for almost a year or so. My middle son was expelled from not one, but two schools between seventh grade and ninth grade for defiant behavior. By this time, he was running away, getting picked up for petty theft by the police, and ended up on probation. However, that never stopped him. It seems like at least once a week; I was picking him up from the police station for something he had done. If he wasn't being picked up by the police, he was missing for days sometimes weeks at a time. He was only 13 years old at the time. I was completely devastated.

After my mom finished her chemo and semi-recovered from the surgery, she decided that it would be best to move out of our family home, which is where her, my five children, and I had lived for at least ten years or more. The day she moved out was like my world had crashed around me. I felt like I had nothing. My children hated me, my mother didn't want to be in the same home with me, the man I thought loved me walked away, stating he never loved me. My world was crashing and there was nothing I could do about it. I can remember I began to just drink everyday so that I didn't have to feel the pain of abandonment. I didn't have to feel the pain of the evil person I had become. The failure I saw in the mirror was my everyday reality. This is what I thought to be the worst time of my life, little did I know, becoming an alcoholic wouldn't make life any easier or better.

I can remember my middle son came home one day from being missing for over a week, of course at this point I am so mad at him I don't know what to do. I remember giving him a bunch of chores to do and I can remember right before I black out him saying to me, "Bi*** I aint doing sh**." The next thing I knew, my then 14-year-old son and I were fighting like a real deal fist fight, and he was literally fighting back. It was so bad my own son tried to kick me down a flight of stairs to the concrete basement. I don't remember exactly how the fight broke up, but I do remember him running out of the front door and me not seeing him again for another week or so.

With all this going on in my home, my mother and I were not really talking because being selfish, I thought my mother had abandoned me. I thought she had left me to fail at this thing called "life." I was so angry at her, I was angry at my kids, I was angry at life. I wanted life to simply end....

At this point, my baby girl was no older than my year and a half old baby. One day in April of 2013, I decided that I would just end it all. I wrote a letter to my oldest children telling them that despite all that has happened, I loved them and only wanted what was best for us all. I explained to them that life for me was done and I couldn't take anymore sorrow or hurt. I wrote an addition note for my oldest daughter, telling her to take custody of her younger sister and to make sure her youngest brother went to live with his dad. I explained to her that her middle brother could be turned over to the state or simply stay in the streets where he had been all this time. I pulled my firearm from the safe, I pulled the hydrocodone pills from the bottle, poured a tall glass of vodka to wash down the pills, loaded the firearm, placed the firearm in my lap, and took the first set of pills. After swallowing the first set of pills, my daughter came into my room demanding that she was hungry, I called my middle son over and over again for him to come get her, but he wouldn't answer me. When I went downstairs, I was so mad because he wouldn't answer, but I found him in his bed sleep, which is still odd because even in their sleep my children always answered me. By this time I am feeling a little weird because the pills and liquor have kicked in, I put a hotdog in the microwave for one minute, take the hotdog out, cut it into pieces (she is only 1.5 years old, so I couldn't give it to her whole), now I am calling my daughter to come downstairs to the kitchen to eat so that I can go upstairs and finish what I started. My daughter never comes down, I called her maybe four or five times, my house is not that big, its maybe eleven or so stairs to my upper level so it's not like she couldn't hear me. I go up the stairs so mad at this point that I want to whip her and my son for being blatantly defiant and not listening. I get up the stairs, look around, and she is in her bed sleep. I look around again and the pills and the glass of liquor is over in the garbage. At that very moment all I could do was fall to my knees and ask, "God what is it that you need me to do? Lord have Your way in my life because I am completely weak and weary and there is no more that I can take. Lord have Your way in my life. Show me how to make it through all of this."

I wish I could tell you it was peaches and cream after that, but it wasn't. It took work, prayer, fasting, and a whole lot of praising my way through. However, my relationship with my children I made an intentional decision to mend, the relationship with my mother, I made an intentional decision to mend, she has beat breast cancer and colon cancer at this point. She was diagnosed with colon cancer maybe two years after the breast cancer battle. No, these relationships didn't mend easily, but they also didn't fall apart easily. It took work. My youngest son ended up moving with his dad, I moved to St. Louis, Missouri, and my middle son ended up in the juvenile detention center and a rehabilitation center for two years, after being taken out of the home and placed in foster care by the court system.

I stand today as an International motivational speaker, a two-time Amazon best-selling author. I have a successful not for profit organization and tour (based on personal testimonies of up to 20 different men and women). Although my middle son is back in jail; he came home for about a year and a half before he was back in jail again, life is truly good for me. My children and have an amazing relationship, my mom and I are the best of friends... Life is good! When things get challenging, which they will, I don't give up, I look up. The Scripture that pulls me through and allows me to not only help myself but help others as well is: *Habakkuk 2 New King James Version (NKJV) The Just Shall Live by Faith,* **2** *I will stand my watch, And set myself on the rampart, And watch to see what He will say to me, And what I will answer when I am corrected.* [2] *Then the Lord answered me and said: "Write the vision, And make it plain on tablets, That he may run who reads it.* [3] *For the vision is yet for an appointed time; But at the end it will speak, and it will not lie. Though it tarries, wait for it; Because it will surely come, It will not tarry.* [4] *"Behold the proud, His soul is not upright in him; But the just shall live by his faith.*

www.mikkitamoore.com

info@mikkitamoore.com

www.artoftransparency.org

info@artoftransparency.org

Part 3 - YOU CAN SOAR

The Treatment and After Care of Failure

By Jutoria Aaron

The Disease: Failure

Throughout my life, I always wanted to be the best at everything I did. I wanted to be the best in school. I wanted to be the best at dancing. I even wanted to be the best at sports. Here is the thing, I was good in school, but not the best. The only dance I really knew how to do was the holy step. And believe it or not, I only was good at volleyball, but didn't take it all the way to college because of the mandatory 5:00 a.m. workouts. I wanted to be the best at everything, so much so that I became depressed when I failed. I can now admit that failure was my kryptonite, and the longer it took me to address it, the deeper I fell into a never-ending cycle of incompletion. I was stuck, sinking deeper into the quicksand. I was stumbling as my knees became victimized by the load on my shoulders. My ears were ringing, agitated from the cries that only they could hear. All of this because of my past failures, which paralyzed me. But now, I can proclaim that I am a survivor of the disease that infest the bodies and souls of so many. It's called, "Fear of Failing." This is a crippling disease that hinders one's mind from seeing and obtaining success. It blocks one's vision from seeing their wings to fly. Over time, it deteriorates the nucleus of dreams.

Failure had imprinted itself in my mind, and when I think about it, fear of failing was based on the statistics and generational curses that held my family and friends hostage for so long. I had to break them. I had to break them. There is no question about it, but realizing that I had wings to fly, fear of failing stopped me from jumping. It was only when I realized it was disabling me that I knew something had to be done. One day I looked failure straight in the eyes and hugged it. I held it so tight. I rubbed my hand across its face and admired its beauty. I realize I had to ADDRESS the disease in order to ADJUST to it. Adjusting to failure or the fear of failing isn't easy. Adjusting to failure requires one to know it is inevitable, but the reaction and recovery from it is what will determine how prosperous your life is. Someone can have nothing of their own, and be the happiest because they have not crucified themselves to failure. Here I will talk about how I addressed and adjusted to failure, and it is my prayer that something is said that will encourage you to put one foot in front of the other, for it is only then will you walk into your destiny.

Address and Adjust: Make It Your Own!

Let me say that truthfully, I didn't overcome failure. It became a part of me. To overcome something is to defeat it. Now, when dealing with failure, this ideology may allow some to think that failure is something you only have to address once, and if you defeated it before, then you'll never have to address it again. This thinking is a set up. I hearten you not to say you defeated failure, but you owned failure, for it is something that you will have to address and adjust to continuously.

Owning something gives you the power to do what you please with it. So, I ask you, what will you do with your failure? Will you own it? Will you die from the disease of fear of failing? Are you willing to put your name on failure? Are you ready to address it?

When you are the boss of something, you are able to tell that something what to do and where to go. When you are in ownership of something, you also have the ability to adjust it to your benefit. Think on this. There is a story in the Bible that can be found in the eighth chapter of John. Here, Jesus was in

Jerusalem, and He entered an area where the sick had laid until an angel came down to trouble the waters. When the waters were troubled, the sick could enter the pool and be made whole. The Bible speaks of a man who had been sick for over thirty-five years who couldn't get to the water. Jesus healed him and then told him to pick us his bed and walk. I often wondered why Jesus told him to pick up something he had been bound to for so long. Then it came to me, Jesus was giving the man power to address what had him bound, so that he could adjust it for good. Like Jesus told the man to pick up his bed and walk, I am encouraging you to pick up your failure and fear of failing and strut your stuff. Walking with your failure forces you to address it, and in the midst of your walking, you can adjust it for your good. Who knows? Sometimes you may have to lean on failure like a walking cane. Or use failure as a letter to get you to a higher level. This is a way you can turn the purpose *of* something into the purpose *for* something. What was meant to enslave you shall now be used as the doorpost of your liberty. Use your failures. Walk with them. Own them; therefore, you can have the power to adjust them and make them work for you. You are the conductor of your life's composition. Your failure has to obey you. Show it who's boss.

I proclaim that this day you will begin to claim your failures as your own. I decree that what has held you bound will become a sign of triumph. As I continue to reflect on the story in the book of John, I realize that another reason Jesus told the man to pick up his bed and walk was because He wanted the man to always be reminded of what he had been delivered from. To be reminded of something is to remember, when you have to remember, you have to think back on the past. I hearten you to get to a place where you have to be reminded of failure because it no longer can invade your thinking about your present day or your future. IT IS IN THE PAST. So, in your season of adjusting, address failure as an ex occurrence, or a former thing. It wasn't until I owned my failure that I was able to grow and glow. In owning failure, I am now able to address it and adjust to it. In addition to addressing and adjusting to failure I had to come up with a treatment plan to completely overcome failure, no matter how many times it reoccurred.

The Treatment: I can, I did, I will

Once I acknowledged that failure and the fear of failing was something I should embrace and own, I had to come up with a strategy to help survive it. I had to figure out a treatment plan to continuously refute the disease. I came up with a motto. "I can, I did, I will." I embodied this saying so much that I wrote it on my cap when I received my Bachelor's degree. This motto became my treatment. Let me explain. Each sector of the slogan, "I can, I did, I will" is a phase.

I can...

The "I can" phase is the phase you are in at this very moment. The "I can" phase is where you are readily taking on the current responsibilities to make it to the next minute, hour, or day. The I can phase usually involves a lot of self-motivation. "I think I can," or "Okay I got this." How about this one? "If I just make it through one more day of work." It's so common to get lost in this phase as everything in it may seem as though you've become stuck in a routine. This phase also has a lot to do with things that are not in your control. For example, working to pay bills or even worse, working to pay an unexpected bill. But through it all, the "I can" phase starts with the small analysis that whatever it is, you can get through it. The phase of, "I can" is where you have to believe that you are more than capable of doing the activities of today, tomorrow, and the next day. The mind frame that is needed during the phase of "I can" should be of one that is motivated to take the small steps, for they too matter when overcoming failure, or fear of failing. I can stick to a schedule. I can get through another day of work. I can begin to work out. I can make the necessary steps to overcome failure. I can. As cliché as it may be, we all should have the mind frame of the little engine that could; however, instead of screaming, "I think I can! I think I can!" I declare you to scream, "I know I can!" *I know I can do whatever I put my mind to.* On the inside of you dwells a unique, new, and unfamiliar strength. I dare you to introduce yourself to it, and dance with it, step with it, spin it around like a ballerina dancing on a jewelry box. Dance baby dance. The newfound strength that comes out of the, "I can" phase is what will get the ball rolling on overcoming failure. It is what stirs up the conquer in you. The "I can" phase is the perfect time to get to know your greatest strength; for it is that, that will walk you into the doors of the "I did" phase.

I did...

I call this phase the "I did" phase because it comes after you have completed something. It's the phase after everything on the checklist, for the moment, is done. It's the time when the goal is achieved, or what you've thirst for has been obtained. In this phase, you should be proud, for it is here where you've won your first round with failure. I personally like the "I did" phase. It's when one realizes they have some triumphs under their belt. For example, I bask in the ambiance of the "I did" phase when I received my Bachelor's degree. It was something I set out to do and it came to pass. My I cans turned into I did. It is here when you get a little taste of success. It's when you feel one step closer to self-actualization and overall fulfilment; however, I warn you of its side effects. A dosage of the "I did" phase can be vigorous to winning the second round with failure.

Why?

I'm glad you asked.

When in the "I did" phase one gets a little taste of accomplishment; therefore, they may become complacent with where they are in life. The "I did" phase is where you are able to see your progress. You are able to see how far you've come. It is in this phase where you may even compare some of the things you've achieved to your peers or others your age, and/ or in your position. In the "I did" phase you can become comfortable, but as I am writing this, I warn you to not become friends with comfortability. With comfortability comes a lackadaisical spirit. In comfortability, one can become blind to the greater things, for even the best can become better. Take this for intense. As I stated before, I received my Bachelor's degree. The "I can," turned into I did, but that was years ago. I graduated in 2018. I looked around at my former peers and realized I had a better grip on life than some; however, I have still become a prisoner to comfortability. I thought I would go right on to get my Master's, and even obtain a doctorate degree. It was only when I realized that I was not overcoming failure, but sustaining in it. I knew more had to be done, and even though I haven't gone back to school yet, I have become aware of this costume that fear of failing disguised itself in.

As we are continuously overcoming failure, and the fear of failing, it is important to remember that failure is something that is always sneaking up on us. I once heard: "When you go to a higher level, you must fight a different devil." This means, you must keep fighting and pressing to a higher level. I want you to know that the "I did" phase is truly a frenemy. It's both good and bad. Yes, you made it happen, but you made it happen for the time of yesterday. Once you get this in your head, you will find yourself thinking higher, and becoming higher simultaneously. So, I encourage you to always make it happen for today, tomorrow, and ever more. See yourself as higher. See yourself as being able to do anything. Never let anyone tell you that you can't fly. And if they do, send them a picture of a plane ticket. You can do more, so celebrate in the I did phase, but don't hesitate to leave it. You can, for yesterday. You did, for today. And tomorrow you will.

I will...

The "I will" phase is what is the most important. Now that you know that you can, and you have celebrated what you did, it is now time to plan the next goal. One can fail at failing to prepare. Habakkuk 2: 2-3 "Write down the revelation and make it plan on tablets so that a herald may run with it. For the revelation awaits an appointed time; it speaks of the end and will not prove false. Though it lingers, wait for it; it will certainly come and will not delay." This mean whatever you plan to do, write it down simple enough so that you can obtain the vision and go back to the plan at any time. If it is worth it, it is worth the time and the process. To achieve what you want at its best; you must go through a process. This process includes planning.

A lot of people remain hostages of failure because they refuse to go through the process in the "I will" phase. The "I will" phase is where you should begin to brainstorm. A perfect example of something that pertains to the "I will" phase is a vision board. Vision boards are helpful as they work as visual planners, but too many people are entertained by the physical properties they hold. They want to make them pretty and flashy. I am sorry to tell you, but your planning is supposed to be messy. You're supposed to have things scratched off, marked up, and annotated. All plans need revision as well. Unfortunately, life never goes as planned; therefore, leave room for error and mistakes. If you prepare for them, then you can formulate a combative formula for the disease of failure. You have the keys to unlock the doors of opportunity, but you have to plan to do so. "Proper preparation prevents poor performance" in all situations. Do not be a witness to the reign of failure. Begin to write out your goals. Even if they seem minor. A goal for me today was to get up the on the first alarm versus hitting snooze, and I did it. This means tomorrow I will do it because I planned to do it before and succeeded. Plan that vision out. Plan that book out. Plan for that business. You will receive what God has for you. You will achieve the goals you set. You will acquire supernatural abilities to run the race set before you. You will be the lender and not the borrower. You will be the head and not the tail. You will be the king and queen of your household. You will overcome generational curses. You will overcome abuse. You will overrule the chains of systematic oppression. You will overcome failure. Why? Because you planned for it.

The After Care: Find Your Place on the Spectrum!

It is important to see that the "I can" and the "I did" are both referring to things of the past. Both phases put emphasis of achievement whether they are big or small. The "I will" phase gives hope, and room for one to dream and reach levels never seen before. As you go on and invest in you, I want you to think of the three phases I explained as being on a spectrum. It is important to see the treatment of failure as being on a spectrum because it emphasizes how fluent the phases are. It doesn't matter where your starting point is after reading this. You may already be in the "I did" phase. You've made some dreams a reality. You've won the second round with failure and now you are planning the next thing for you to do. Everything you aspire to do you can do it, just find out where you are on the spectrum. Some of you may be at the very beginning of the treatment process. You may be at the beginning of the spectrum in the "I can" phase. You fight with failure every day and press your way to make it through. If this is you, keep fighting it, and before you know it, you'll find yourself entering a new phase and discovering new abilities on the spectrum.

Remember in overcoming failure, you first have to address it and adjust to it. Call it by name, and don't sugarcoat it. Continue the treatment in overcoming the disease. The phase of, "I can" will purge you. The phase of, "I did" will prepare you. The phase of, "I will" shall propel you. Do not submit to failure. It shall not win. To continue to be the victor of failure, you must keep up on the spectrum. Where are you now, and where are you headed? I decree that the disease of failure cannot have your ministry. Declare that the disease of fear of failing will not overtake your dreams. You shall live and not die. You shall walk and not faint. I pray these words bring comfort in your pressing, confidence in purpose, and calmness in your process. You shall live in your truth. You can. You did. You will. You can. You did. You will. You Can...

jutoriaaaron@gmail.com

"When are you going to go home?"

By Daria Rosen

Have you ever had words spoken to you that felt as if you had been sucker punched in the stomach? That question, innocently uttered by my mother, disturbed me to my core and was the impetus to a journey that finds me here and you reading these words.

To truly understand the magnitude of these words and the impact they had, I must share the back story.

I am an only child. Wipe most of the negative perceptions away that you have about only children and that's me. I am loved a lot, not spoiled. I am take charge, not bossy. Well, maybe a little bit. I have learned to share. The latter is not a skill that one has to practice when there is no one to share with. Seeing others succeed gives me joy and I am quite comfortable being the sideline cheerleader or efficiently in the background. I cannot tell you how many times I've said to my family, "I only want to do my job and be incognito." My mother's response has always been "You are an almost six foot tall black woman, you are going to be noticed." Attention makes me uncomfortable. As a pianist for choirs and accompanist for others, I love playing behind a tall upright piano or when on a grand piano, positioning the lid so those watching or listening cannot see me.

The desire to be incognito extended into my corporate career, however, the Lord has a good sense of humor. Luke 12:48 in its entirety reads 'But he that knew not, and did commit things worthy of stripes, shall be beaten with few stripes. For unto whomsoever much is given, of him shall much be required; and to whom men have committed much, of him they will ask the more.'

Remember the trait of taking charge mentioned above? My father excelled at taking charge, getting things done and in his career of quality control, how to call out ambiguity and ineptness. Like father. Like daughter.

Although desiring anonymity and being incognito, I always questioned what was wrong or spoke up for others and typically, unknown to me because I never cared about titles, the individuals that I addressed where people of power or position. My father's trait and the skills and talents I was blessed with allowed me to work closely with C-suite executives, manage division budgets, lead company-wide programs, and speak to audiences in the hundreds.

This trait has landed me in trouble with some managers and appreciated by others. The latter is how I ended up in the IT Medical field leading teams to implement electronic medical record systems in numerous hospitals and later clinics. The expertise gained is how I became a consultant in this field and was the impetus to my mother's comment.

For several years, each week on Sunday afternoon or evening, I flew to the client's location and returned home Thursday evenings. Her question angered me, and my response was, "I am home." She pointed out that I spent more time with the clients than my loved ones. That stopped me in my tracks. She was right.

Scheduling friends for breakfast, lunch or dinner plans on Fridays was how I kept tied to those at home. One Friday, dinner was an invitation to a party that was also a business opportunity meeting. I wanted to spend time with my girlfriend so I said sure.

Once there, the product intrigued me because it was simple and would not change my minimal and somewhat laughable night routine. It was however the business opportunity that caught my eye and I thought, *Hmmm, this is something that would allow me income to stay at my real home with my husband and parents.* So, I signed up.

I attained minimal success; yet, I let those that did not have the same vision as I cause me to doubt myself and believe that I could not build a business. They do not pay my bills, yet their opinions became more important than my loved ones.

The Scripture quoted earlier says "to whom much is given much is required." I was blessed with many talents, skills; yet, I was sitting on them. Another Scripture tells the story about a man that buried his talent and when the owner returned and found the talent, it had not been utilized, it was taken away and given to someone else.

Fear, false evidence appearing real, was holding me back and a vise of doubt and lack of belief in myself held me firmly rooted in place and becoming more disbelieving. A vicious circle.

I joined an online group of broadcasting women to force myself to speak to an unknown world audience. *Who's watching? What are they thinking? Are they going to like me?* I needed to do something to break through this petrifying fear and as mentors have said, "Be Visible!" Each time I pressed the red button, I became more confident and less worried about what those watching thought. Like a caterpillar transforming into a butterfly, those skills and talents that were buried and encased began to reemerge.

There are thirty two other authors, some new, some seasoned in this book. I was number thirty three. Why? Because I did not believe my words would make a difference so I hesitated in participating.

Remember my business? For a while it appeared to be more of a hobby than a business. Something clicked as the New Year was approaching and I realized that I allowed others to pray over my business, yet I did not pray over my business. So I began. I was not satisfied with results because I was not satisfied with my efforts. I made the decision to believe in myself. I made the decision to utilize my God-given talents. They are mine! That's an only child thing. My business is exploding. Partners are joining, customers are calling, and I am having fun!!

Thank you, mother, for asking, "When are you going to go home?" I'm here and I am visible.

What is causing you to not believe in yourself? Be like the caterpillar, go through the struggle and emerge as a glorious butterfly. You Can!

Website: www.dariarosen.com

Email: daria@dariarosen.com

Five Must Know Benefits for People of Color Investing in Real Estate

By Marcus Carter

The majority of my readers who utilize and subscribe to discovering their success language, while anomalies are rampant, fall into a simple category: they want more. They are analytical, damn near surgical in their movement, and view success as a habit that can be nurtured and cultivated. Money is not a goal but a method (think about that and let that sink in). They've deduced and calculated how they are going to position themselves and create a life of their own design. I am them, you are too. The articulation of my personal success language led me into a particular place that on the path to creating wealth is unavoidable, real estate.

The business of leveraging real estate to create wealth, if not in practice, yet and still in observance of how to leverage real estate; basically, you need to understand real estate on many levels, whether you activate on it or not. While I'm passionate about an opportunity to figure out the puzzle that is investing in real estate, I'm not per se passionate about real estate. Put simply, the margins are better. A person will work everyday regards of what their profession or wage is. And if you're going to work anyway, might as well get paid. Checking the margins are essential. The stress levels of real estate can be a hazard, but to a person with a well-articulated success language, the margins make it worth it. The ends justify the means. The margins are good. Real estate, when properly positioned, is far less risky of an investment than other traditional investment strategies like stocks and bonds.

A reader with a success language that points in the direction of real estate to grow wealth utilizes all of the components at their disposal; heart, hustle, and muscle. The automatic predisposition to real estate, if not in allure, then definitely a rational deduction on how to take part in a mechanism that can dramatically impact just about every aspect of a person's life. Said individual with a well-articulated success language has a path outlined internally and understands real estate's multi-level impact. Said individual is not in it for the job, but for the income. Wealth is the main symbol of social stratification. Real estate is the true representation of the urban legend described as the American Dream, the most logical way for a person of meager means to explore wealth, freedom, and social impact quickly, effectively, efficiently in a rapid fashion. Let's go further with this. Let's talk about the five must know benefits of investing in real estate.

Community

For people of color in the United States, there is an adamant stance that voices are not heard. The limitations for people of color when it comes to proper representation is illustrated in the weaponized public policy used to maintain and ultimately control. As it was at the beginning in this country, owning land makes the landowners voice undeniable. The slivery ways of politicians, whom wax poetically about commitments to the disenfranchised, don't seem to let down the wealthy when it comes to fighting for their constituents. People of color are often looked at as welfare recipients and a population that is looking for a handout. This could not happen if we "owned the block." Politicians who legislate public policy would be forced to listen. Politicians, while at times unsavory, are not idiots, they know who they have to appease. While real estate is commonly associated with wealth and financial freedom, it provides even more language when it comes establishing a power base in the community. Gentrification, redlining, and a host of other tactics in place to stymie ownership by people of color can be thwarted through efficient and strategic real estate investment strategies.

Employment

Everybody, and I mean everybody seems to daydream about being their own boss. That is until after they actually become the boss. As one of the majority of African Americans that have a college degree that has to rationalize the debt accumulated for a degree not used and shamed into working to payback this debt, which ultimately serves as a catalyst for generational financial slavery. America itself is built on leveraging debt. Endless assembly lines of employees with nothing to show for their toil but an ever-increasing wealth gap and one percent that they enrich. Work is work no matter how you choose to perform it, my thought has always been, might as well work diligently on your own pursuits. For all those daydreaming in a cubicle about taking more control of the work they do, real estate as a business is instant credibility. About the only thing more instantaneous from a credibility standpoint is becoming an author.

Risk Aversion

As humbly as I can possibly say, the American way is built on the idea of getting something for nothing. We annexed America from the Native Americans, and anointed this the land of the free. We offered a better life where there were no ceilings. We duped ourselves into believing this. Today is an overwhelming rush of options to indulge in short sighted wealth attempts, and the allure of getting rich is more alive than ever. Network marketing, Shark Tank, the Kardashians, athletes and rappers. You can get on with anything and dreams are sold daily. This has not blemished the reputations of grandfathered institutions like the stock market and an overall American aversion to entrepreneurship. But every lane I've mentioned carries its own considerable amount of risk. Real estate itself is a risky venture. But I'd argue incompetence is the biggest infraction investors face. A savvy investor can weather the storms of the economy as land is a nonrenewable resource. They're not making anymore. Stock markets crash, consumers can be fickle, the world can be unkind, athletes and Instagram models age, but real estate. Real estate marches on, not without consequence, but as stable and efficient as you can find in this crazy mixed-up world we live in.

Wealth Creation

I'm not a genius, but I'm considered to be a fairly intelligent man. Money, which even an idiot might know, is a standard bearer of status and freedom. Much of life is dominated by fear. Money is not the cure, but it helps. Let's be real, who dreams of a life of meager means. I don't care how much substance a person is mired in, nobody daydreams of being broke. Most of us struggle to appreciate and understand that we are lucky to be breathing. No matter where we are in life, we do daydream about having more. For whatever reason, for the status, the fame, the fortune, or even just to give it back, we are all drawn to the allure of amassing wealth. Real estate is riding a pretty obvious wave as the pop culture embraces REI (Real Estate Investing). Fix and flip shows are everywhere and training programs to teach REI sometimes command into the six-figures. Why? People want in and no matter the embellishment, it is true. Real estate is the only true get rich quick scheme that actually works. Again, incompetence is the biggest culprit. Real Estate can change your life over night without even the slightest hint of luck.

Flexibility

In my time in real estate, I've yet to meet an individual that wasn't curious. I do my best to take time out to share what I know with whomever has questions. I don't sugarcoat anything, it's a jungle out there, but there is a method to the madness. Success, as with your success language, can be engineered. Markets change, but real estate, and the leverage of real estate is not going anywhere. This means there is a tremendous amount of flexibility. The game will be here next year and the year after. Although it may be argued if wealth and financial freedom is what an individual is seeking, why wait? But if it isn't your season, then it just isn't your season. You can become a realtor. Keep your job or quit. Cash flow or flip. New York to California. Pay cash or get financing. A real estate investment strategy can be customized to you. I don't know any other form of wealth creation that allows for you to generate wealth on your own terms.

Real estate definitely has its benefits. More so than others possibly, but it is still a job. It's glamorous, but comes with tremendous risk. As with any other venture, commitment, discipline, patience, and diligence are benchmarks. While the virtue of the wealth creation possible regulated by generous margins is enough to trigger even the most timid, the possible financial pitfalls are just as rampant. You can have the amazing six-figure payday, but also must defend against the six-figure bath you take on a real estate miscalculation. So you must be strong! You can!

marcuscarter.writer@gmail.com

312.273.3487

My Journey to Freedom

By Darrick Campbell

As a writer, the most difficult part is how to begin and structure your thoughts. As I spoke with my writing coach, she helped me with my creative juices and remind me about the importance of this project. As the world struggles with the COVID-19 Pandemic and stay-at-home orders seem to be extended every week, most people feel trapped, isolated, and other emotions they didn't even know they felt. I was viewing the news one morning, and I watched as the anchor equated his experience with the pandemic to being a prisoner and his freedom ripped from him. In that moment, it came to me as to what I wanted to contribute to this project. I wanted to write about how on a daily basis, I wanted to live my freedom. When I mention freedom, it is most certainly not the kind people most think of. The freedom I mean, is the freedom of self and the freedom of the mind.

Freedom starts in the mind. In the movie, *Shawshank Redemption*, which in my opinion, is one of the greatest movies ever made, Andy Dufresne, played by Tim Robbins, embarks on a life sentence after he was convicted of killing his wife and her lover. What makes the movie so profound for me, is that the movie seems to be entirely about the horrors of prison. But for me, it is not about prison at all. Andy transitioned mentally out of the place the moment he arrived. His body may have been in prison, but his mind was elsewhere. Just like with meditation, he blocked out all the noise and focused his mind to where he should be, where he needed to be. When the time was right, he manifested his thoughts and he was successfully able to escape.

Andy had Kind thoughts, perseverance and focus; his mind was always free.

So, how did I start my journey to Freedom of The Mind? You may be surprised that it started with fasting. Yes, for the past three years, I use Mondays to fast. It is very difficult to articulate the profound benefits it does for my body and mind. No other time during the week do I feel close to GOD than I do on Mondays. Fasting, forces me to engage my thoughts, solve problems, and think of things in their entirety. I have learned if I could control my hunger, I could control many other aspects of my life. So many believe fasting is difficult, and it is. If you're trying it for the first time, start by fasting for a few hours and then gradually moving it up. After a few weeks, you will see and feel what I feel. During the fast, take time to acknowledge your faith, meditate, and read things that feeds your life and purpose. Another great thing about fasting, it does wonders for those trying to lose weight.

"Never looking back or too far in front of me, the present is a gift and I just want to be." These words are expressed by the great Rapper and Actor, Common. He has driven me to simply, "BE." The state of being or freedom of self for me is, a personal, truthful, and spiritual space within oneself. The process started for me when I would constantly allow people to control my emotions. This aggravated me so much that I started to seek out ways to control it. I was already fasting, praying, and meditating, but something was still holding me back from the freedom I so coveted. As an avid reader, something told me to reread, *The Alchemist*. If you have not heard or read this book, shame on you (kidding). I am not going to tell you much about it, but I will say, you will enjoy it immensely. So, I started to really focus on my emotions and who had access to them. I did two things that changed my outlook forever. First, I stopped trying to get people to understand my point of view. I started to be completely clear and concise with my words and if the person didn't agree or understand, that simply was not my issue. Second, which was a difficult one, was to stop having expectations of people. I completely stopped giving people the opportunity to let me down. The letdown, most of the time, was very painful and ruined relationships. I had to protect my peace; my freedom depended on it.

There you have it. A small preview of my Journey to freedom. Every day, I start the morning with meditation. During that time, I asked God and the Universe for the things I need to be sustainable, the things which bring me peace. Some things are delivered, and some things are not. Yet, my journey continues. If you are ready to be free, now is the time to start searching out the things that can help you achieve that. If fasting is too severe, or meditation is not your thing, try reading, *The 7 Spiritual Laws of Success* by Deepak Chopra. It is a short read, but packs so much substance. I am sure you will enjoy it.

Focusgroup1980@gmail.com

Connect The Dots

By Nicole Lofton

I always would say to myself: *I will accomplish everything I set out to do.* This has stuck with me over the years. However, I include God in everything I set out to do. Therefore, His will can be done. I believe that God will place something in our hearts to lead us to where we need to be. There are many things that happen while on that path.

The hardest part about accomplishing what you set out to do is, trusting the process. This means you may not always have support, you may have doubters, you may even doubt yourself, but you cannot let that stop you. For years, I had things I wanted to accomplish. I had dreams and goals, but I also had self-doubt, low self-esteem, and a lack of support. I also fell into the trap of allowing other people to define what success was for me, and I believe many people also fall into this trap.

So first, let's start there, when it comes to success, never let anyone define that for you. Success looks different for everyone. People tend to look at what others are doing and then internalize it as they themselves are not as successful. I am here to tell you that if you set a goal and accomplish it, that is success. Now, why would I say something like that? I know that most times we hear cliché statements and opinions. One of them is, a goal is nothing if you never do anything with it.

Now of course, for the most part, that is true. However, setting a goal can be successful. Let's say you are a person who just never set a goal in your life. Let's say you never really had anything you wanted to accomplish, but once you really thought about it, there was something deep down you wanted. So, you set a goal, that is success. There are people who never set goals because they are not motivated, because they feel like they have no value to add, or they do not feel that they have a purpose.

I am speaking to those people right now. God has placed something inside of you and it is for you. This thing you may view as a hobby. You might like to paint, sing, draw, you may even have a heart for children. It's the things we view as hobbies or "not that interesting" that we should be doing. We have this view because we are allowing others to define to us what success is. We even allow people to tell us what working looks like and to some people it certainly doesn't look like entrepreneurship (but for me it does).

There is power in not only setting goals, but also writing them down. I can personally tell you even in this moment, there are goals that I wrote down five years ago that are just now happening. One of my goals was to be a writer. I don't view it as a goal, I view it as something I set out to accomplish, it's my heart's desires. So, I would rather use my heart's desires, rather than goals.

I fell in love with writing when I was in the fourth grade. It was then I learned about different poets such as Maya Angelou and Langston Hughes, and I have been writing poetry ever since. However, I never really had the confidence. Even though I would get recognized for my writing, like the time in fourth grade when my letter got sent to the president and then again in high school after September 11th when we had to write a letter to the president and mine was one that was chosen. It still didn't mean much to me because I didn't have anyone close to me that would show interest or encourage me in that area or any area. Until one day, one of my college professors said to me, "You know I always love reading your writing, you are a really good writer, you should continue writing." I was surely surprised, because she never said much to me and we were just passing each other in the hallway, but it did mean a lot to me. However, it didn't move me to write. I knew in college, I was writing so that I could pass whatever class I was taking.

I am telling this story to show how things tie into each other, because God is always working behind the scenes. I graduated from college with my Bachelor's Degree in Psychology in 2007 and in 2008, I entered an abusive relationship (smooth transition, right?) I was also in graduate school at the time, pursuing a Master's Degree in Marriage and Family Counseling, which I did not finish. However, once I got out of that situation and I discovered what domestic violence was, I became an anti-domestic violence advocate. My dad also encouraged me to start a domestic violence blog, so I did. That was a life-changing experience. I met so many people and connected with so many other advocates and survivors who are still a part of my life to this day. That moment was when I finally started to feel purpose in my life and I knew there was more to it. I always wanted to start a nonprofit, so I started one to educate and raise awareness on issues such as domestic violence and mental health. That wasn't what I originally wanted my nonprofit to be focused on, but God had other plans.

My point is, God will give you the desires of your heart according to His will (the HIS will part is important). He encourages us to write the vision and make it plain. He tells us that the reason we don't have certain things is because we haven't asked. This is not about material things, although He will do that too, this is more about purpose. What is in your heart? Pay attention to do that because God, more than likely, put it there! What experiences have you had in life? Pay attention because pain has purpose.

That is why I am an advocate, author, and a certified Christian life coach.

Info@purposewhispers.com

www.purposewhispers.com

Flow

By Tammy C. Francis, Ph.D.

Decisions were difficult for me, especially major life decisions. So, when I found myself at a crossroads, I would know it and feel it, but I would have a difficult time making a decision, making a move. So if it was a decision about school, relationships, purchases, trips, among many others, I would hesitate, ponder, and overthink. Then, I would miss the opportunity. In all honesty, this still happens occasionally.

Lately, the pull in the direction of more and living out the vision for my life is intensifying. I feel that there is more I should be doing. There is more I am meant to do. Initially, I wanted to fight it. I wanted to ignore it. I was torn. I didn't want to reflect. I didn't want to admit it. I didn't want to address it. I just didn't. During the 2020 global pandemic, the time at home created an opportunity to reflect on my vision for the future--to admit I am not doing enough and there is more for me to do, like BIG, BIG. Y'all the pull has been so strong lately that I have felt paralyzed. I have felt overwhelmed. And once again, I refused to make a decision to figure it out. I refused to confront the idea I was in the middle of a shift happening in the midst of this global shift and reset.

However, I had to evaluate my thinking and what is holding me back. I had to step back and acknowledge what was going on. There was resistance. Resistance is internal, so I had to acknowledge that too. We like to blame this resistance on things outside of us, outside forces. But no, it is internal. The resistance was coming from me and only me. Why? What was it that I was feeling? I had to pause and take a moment to reflect.

I was being called for greater. Greater than what I was doing. Greater than I envisioned. Greater than what I was planning. Greater than what I was living. So what do I do? [SILENCE] Then, the words I tell or rather chant over and over to my community went off in my head. "FOLLOW THE FLOW!" Don't resist. Just flow with life.

The resistance happens because we are doing things that are not in alignment and doing those things that are going against the direction of what's next for you. Our inability to make a decision (or decisions) comes from that resistance from within. Resistance which is out of the flow for you and what has been designed and designated for you--and waiting for you. Release and allow your next moves to be guided by the flow of your life, your experience. All that was orchestrated in your life has led you to this moment. This moment is a transition which will push you into and transform you for what's next.

When you are desiring more but cannot seem to move forward, there are some steps you can follow to create action and flow.

1. **F**ind the feelings that exists within. Pause and acknowledge what you are feeling.

2. **L**ook at the decisions and experiences that have contributed to those feelings.

3. **O**bserve where the resistance is coming from and at which point in the process do you feel it most.

4. **W**rite down what you have uncovered and discovered when you find, look, and observe. Then reflect on what emerges, the trends and patterns. Write it down!

This reflection will begin the process to determine the resistance occurring and deciding the best option for you at this moment. There is something more for you, right now. It is only revealed when you acknowledge that fact. Then, you must be willing to do something about it. No action, no more. Some action, some more. We should always be moving in the direction of more and preparing for what's next, which is the goal of my brand and businesses. There is more for you. Claim it. You're being called for greater. Embrace it. Follow the flow of life.

info@c4cglobal1.com

www.linktr.ee/DrTammyFrancis

DrTammyFrancis.com

Bliss Bits: Daily Motivation Tools

By Heather Karwacki

It all started when I decided to pick myself up from being down. From reading self-help books, to following motivational leaders, to learning to stop punishing myself for what I thought I did wrong, or was doing wrong in life. It is now known as my, "Bliss bits of inspiration and motivation," usually done on the occasional live broadcast. It has become its own thing and I am proud of it and of myself too. I am by nature a fair introverted person. So, putting myself out there and being received as well as I have been, is inspiring. I mean me, Heather, inspiring people. Wow! If I can, I fully believe you can, too.

You are your story to share. You do not have to bear your soul, just share bits of you, every day. The key is to keep it as productive as possible and maybe a lesson in life from the day or the week. I tend to share emotional wellness tips, breathing exercises, fitness tips, and sometimes nutrition. Whatever sparks me that day in those areas of my passion, I share on it. I am also a Believer, so I may share from time to time on my King, my Savior Jesus. He is my rock. The key is to be you, even if someone else shares on the same topic. You can share, too. You can speak to someone in the world who need to hear your words. Perfection is in progress, so just press record on your phone, or save on your keyboard. Never discount or dilute your thoughts.

Thoughts become dreams, dreams become goals, and goals with a plan become creation.

Thoughts are powerful, I wake up each day with gratitude. No matter my immediate mood, I remind myself that God opened my eyes for this new day, and I am immediately thankful. This is where my Bliss Bits come into flow, the morning mindset. How you wake up mood wise puts your whole mindset in motion for the day. I check my thoughts and reflect in the afternoon, sometimes with a quick minute or two of prayer, self-forgiveness, asking God to forgive and always more gratitude. Then in the evening... You get the idea. It is a habit-forming process, but it is possible. Be open to receive, but also to give. You are a light, a star in the beautiful words sky. Let it be visible.

Remember that you are a light, a love, a blessing, and a powerful presence in this world.

I must give a shout out to Joanne Pham, if you do not know who she is, Google or Twitter search the PeriGirls. This community gave me the tools and so many wonderful friendships. I took a baby step into live social media. I am still baby stepping, but I am coming into my own. Always learning and growing. To those ladies, I thank you always as you have blessed me.

heatherkarwackifitness@gmail.com

Facebook: www.fb.com/heatherkarwacki

Instagram: www.instagram.com/heatherkarwacki

Twitter: twitter.com/heatherkarwacki

It is Finished

By Lawon Smith

When I think of a "You Can" moment in my life, a lot of thoughts, flashbacks, and memories flood my mind. However, the one that really stands, out would be going to college and finishing. I got pregnant with my first child before graduating out of high school. June came and I was six months pregnant, it had never crossed my mind that I would not finish high school. The crazy part about that is, I planned the pregnancy. Yes at 17 years old, I decided to get pregnant. My parents had me when they were teenagers, so this played a role in the decision-making process. At the time, my mother was only in her 30's about to become a grandmother. I graduated from high school pregnant, but with honors. My goal was to prove to my dad that the pregnancy would not stop me from reaching my goals. Oh, I forgot to mention I had also moved out my dad's house to live with my boyfriend and still going to school. The expectation was to step into an adult relationship, create a family, and be successful. Nothing was going to get in the way of me proving that I can do all this.

High school graduation happened with the thought of going to college by the time my baby was 5 years old. We can all go to school was my level of thinking because I got a plan. Well, that did not happen. I looked up and I am living in my own apartment with my little family. I turned 18 years old with a six-month-old baby, paying bills, and all the things that adults do. At this point, college seems to be just a dream because of all the stress that came with the lifestyle I had created. There were so many moments of just sadness or happiness I was experiencing. No one could have ever told me that this would have been my life. Caring for my baby brought me comfort, but when he was asleep or content, a door of depression would open. I would hear voices tell me: "Your life is too hard, just give up." "You are not strong enough." "No one cares about you."

One day I got invited to church by at the time, my boyfriend's sister. The church was filled with many of my boyfriend's family members. They were very nice and welcoming. The pastor asked if I wanted to dedicate the boy back to the Lord. I was ignorant to spiritual stuff, but I felt like this would be a positive thing, so I agreed to come back with my little family. We showed up not only to present our child to the Lord, but it was also the day we dedicated our lives to the Lord as well. This was life changing because I was in a very dark place during this time. After the service, we were invited to my son's new godparents' house. We began to spend a lot of time with them and their family at church. It helped us as a young couple. It was not too many more visits to the church until the pastor asked us about getting married.

We got married, and soon after, I got pregnant with my second child. I was only 20 years old, and all I could think about is that I am never going to get to college. My children became my world. I dedicated myself to be the best mother and now wife. Growing up, I did not have examples of healthy relationships, so trying to do better was also a motivating point for me. After all, I was the first grandkid on both sides of my family, so I felt the need to set the bar higher than the last generation. I guess that attitude came from God, even before I knew him. Now I have two children depending on me to care for them. We also became every active in the church, serving, giving, I mean fully committed. College is the last thing on my mind. Things are going well. I'm learning to pray to God, read the Word, and worship in the spirit.

Then in 1997, my world fell apart. I had inquired about getting my tubes tied so that I would not get pregnant again. At the time, I did not meet the requirements. I had to wait until I was 21 years old. Well, guess who showed up after turning 21 with a positive pregnancy test? Yes, with two kids and the plan to go to school when everyone gets old enough to go to school. When the doctor said congratulations, my heart broke in a million pieces and I just cried my eyes out. This overwhelming weight dropped on me and the doctor sat with me for a moment to make sure I was going to be okay. I had to pull myself together quickly. My mind was tormented with the options of an abortion because this was going to my third child and the second child had just turned six months. I felt like I could not go through childbirth again, we could not afford it, I was to young to have so many kids, I was going to be like my mother with eight kids.

Well I decided to keep my baby, but while I was waiting to see the doctor for a prenatal appointment, there was a sign for an opportunity to serve your community. I read the poster board and decided to apply for AmeriCorps. Yes, I was still pregnant but needed a distraction from the way my life was going. This opportunity offered all the things I needed in order to get my life back in control. However, one of the requirements was completing 1500 hours of community serves hours. So, I was pregnant and was due in December, so I needed to work out a plan on how I was going to successfully complete this program. When I interviewed, I had worked out the time off and the extra time that I would commit to in order to fulfill the required hours. They were impressed with me during the interview, I was selected as one of the eight people that would be the first AmeriCorps group in the Austin community. The program focus was maternal child health, so the pregnant mom was not only a billboard of hope.

This program also an awakening hope in my heart. I was able to learn how to become a home visitor, outreach specialist, breastfeeding peer counselor, and so many other trainings to develop the skills I now use today. After completing the program, the first year I had earned grant money for college. Life was still a little crazy now with three kids, so I decided to do a second year, which opened the door for childcare, health insurance, a small income and now leadership development. I was brought back as a team leader to the new group of members. My self-esteem just went through the roof. I was feeling like I can accomplish anything, so the thought of going to college sprung back up in my heart. I remember talking to one of my supervisors about going, and she told me to start with one class. Her words and faith in God moved a mountain out of the way I thought was impossible.

After completing the second year of AmeriCorps, I was offered a job with a not for profit organization that focused on Maternal Child Health as a trainer. I worked there for about 4 years. I was the program coordinator for a teen breastfeeding program. During this time, I had a lot on my plate. Wearing the hat of mom, wife, intercessor, trainer, friend, leader, and so on. When I lost the funding to my program, something in me broke. I felt inadequate, unequipped, a failure, disappointed, betrayed, and many other feelings. During my prayer time I heard God say: *What are you going to do about it?* I was confused because what could I have done was my thought. Well, I started asking questions about funding while I was working at the organization. I was informed about grant opportunities that could help sustain the program. Now my question was, why didn't someone apply for more funding? Well, there was a proposal, but they didn't get approved.

Now I want to know more about the process of writing proposals for grants and other funding opportunities. As the Fund

Development manager began to share the information with me, I felt like I needed more education. So, I resigned a year later and decided to enroll in school to become a nurse. Yep, a nurse because everyone in the organization that were in leadership had nursing degrees, among other things. I remember driving into the college parking lot scared to death. I had never even been inside of a college, but today was the day I was ready to face my fears. When I walked into the front door, I could feel the anxiety rising, sweaty palms, dry mouth, and a million thoughts flood my mind. I stepped on the elevator and headed to the financial aid office and said I need help. I thought: *Please talk to me like a three-year-old so that I can understand what I need to do to become a student.* The young lady was so kind and informational. She walked me through the process at the junior college where I started my college journey. I started the basics classes like English, public speaking, and because I wanted to be a nurse, I had to take biology.

The first semester went well. I was able to complete like three classes. My grades were great. At the same time, we started pastoring a church. I had no idea how much business skills were needed to run a church. The next semester, I went and requested to add some business classes to learn how to make sure the church was administered properly. This led to me failing a chemistry test I had studied for. I prayed to God about this, and I heard Him say: *I do not need a nurse in the Kingdom.* So, I changed my major to business. But that was not getting it, because church was a different kind of business. I received an invitation from a university up north that had a Bachelor of Arts program in Not for Profit Management.

I stepped into the orientation and fell in love with the mission, vision, campus, and staff. When I left that session, I went home and did the application process. I was accepted into the program.

I spent the next three years in the program. When I was almost at the finish mark, I decided I wanted to have a dual degree. Well, I think the grace had lifted off of me for school, because I got a bad grade in a psychology class. I prayed and ask God what is next, He told me to go through the graduation process, I was getting off course. I went to the admissions office and submitted for the next graduation day. May of 2012 was the big day. I graduated with a Bachelors in Not for Profit Management. It was a journey, but God, through it all, made it possible to finish the race. When it looked like this would never happen, God stepped in and began to take the wheel in my life. I am so grateful for all the people that were a part of my support team during this journey. I can truly say I can do all things through Christ which strengthen me.

pipes62009@gmail.com

www.pipesunrestricted.com

www.facebook.com/pipes

Conclusion – Nina Motivates

By now I am sure you know that no matter what comes your way, YOU CAN! As you see, we all have had different walks in life, but we survive and become overcomers. With God on your side, you can get through anything. He is the answer to all of your problems. Turn to Him. Trust Him. Watch Him make a huge impact on your life. Jesus died so you can be forgiven. There is nothing that is too hard for Him. I pray you use this book as a resource for your future. Whenever you go through, turn to the story that can inspire you to get through. Remember, no matter what.....

YOU CAN

Made in the USA
Las Vegas, NV
03 December 2024

13264476R00079